I am what I ate

Benny

I hope
you enjoy
my memories

Maggie Roppa

I am what I ate

A foodie memoir

Maggie Poppa

© Maggie Poppa, 2008

Published by sixtypluspress

November 2008

ISBN 978-0-9560988-0-1

A CIP catalogue record for this book is available from the British Library.

Inside image © Alexander Zhilyaev | Dreamstime.com

Prepared, printed and cover design by:
York Publishing Services Ltd
64 Hallfield Road
Layerthorpe
York YO31 7ZQ
Tel: 01904 431213
Website: www.yps-publishing.co.uk

Prologue

Almost two years ago my partner John and I received horrible, unexpected news. In spite of never having smoked a single cigarette, nor being a regular drinker, he had mouth cancer. In the ensuing weeks and months he underwent major surgery, reconstructing his mouth after removing the cancer and with it half of his tongue. Thankfully he is well now and has very good odds that the dreaded disease will not return. However, life has changed considerably. We used to be known among our circle of friends as the couple who pursued endless gourmet eating experiences. We would spend whatever seemed right at the time to have a new food experience. It was what we did as a hobby. We ate our way around Britain and indeed, Europe and the USA.

John and I had met each other twelve years before via a dining club. I had been alone for two years after the end of a ten-year relationship, and had decided to treat myself to the membership as a birthday gift to me to cheer myself up. It worked. That first evening, when we sat opposite each other at a table in Korks Wine Bar and Restaurant in Otley, was the first of many when we talked endlessly and enjoyed each other's company. Gradually, as we left group dining behind, eating wonderful meals in fabulous restaurants became the way we spent our leisure time; and drinking good wine at home became the norm. That is now a thing of the past as John is only able to eat a very soft diet, without spices or strong flavours, which seem to make his mouth burn, and wine unfortunately tastes like vinegar.

But we often talk about the meals we shared – they are such wonderful memories. I have gradually realised that throughout my life, my memories have been linked to food, and I've often said that one day I would put them down on paper. Now it seems that for the present, new, shared, memorable food experiences will be few and far between, so this is maybe the best time to start my memoir. After all I am what I ate.

1

Visits to the Aunties

Seed cake

½ lb self-raising flour
½ lb sugar
½ lb butter
4 medium eggs
1 oz Caraway seeds
½ teaspoon nutmeg
½ teaspoon ground cinnamon.

1 x 7in round cake tin

Oven gas mark 4 or 350ºF.

Cream butter and sugar together, and add stiffly beaten egg whites, then gradually add the beaten yolks. Gradually fold in flour and spices, before pouring into the greased cake tin and baking for about an hour until golden brown.

This cake keeps well and is even better the second day onwards.

It was the week after Christmas, and Mum was buttoning me into my big coat and wrapping a knitted woollen scarf around my neck. This was the winter visit to see my aunties who lived across the city in Austhorpe, on the eastern outskirts of Leeds. I was excited as always, because firstly seeing the aunties meant another late Christmas present, secondly a long trip on the bus, but most of all it meant lots of different, delicious food.

I knew that when we arrived we would be ushered into one of their two adjoining bungalows for an hour or so of small talk while the families brought each other up to date. Each auntie would be backwards and forwards between the kitchen and the dining room bringing first one plate and then another of something to delight and tempt me. My six-year old eyes would grow rounder with every plateful.

There was Auntie Ethel who was my father's elder sister. In his family he was the lastborn of nine children with Ethel, the eldest, followed by seven brothers, then he himself, Edwin. It was always clear that my Dad had been her favourite, probably because she had a big hand in bringing him up. Ethel was widowed and I have no idea how long before that had happened, as I cannot recall anyone talking of her husband, or seeing any photographs of him, so I'm unable to add any detail about him. The other Auntie we were visiting was Nellie, Ethel's daughter. Together they were a formidable team. They looked like country-born women who had been baking for the WI stall all their lives. Thinking of them now, I could imagine them in a pose for a photograph, each with a clean white pinafore and each with a Victoria sponge or a Dundee cake held proudly, standing in their kitchen and smiling into the camera lens.

Auntie Ethel was rounded and small with fine, permed, white hair which showed the pink of her scalp through the tight, sometimes frizzy, curls. Auntie Nellie was also a very rounded woman but taller and her naturally wavy hair was cut short into the nape of her neck. I always think of her as a laughing lady who hummed a lot as she went about her work. Apparently she had a beautiful soprano voice and was much in demand in the weeks before Christmas as a soloist in local performances of "Messiah". They both smelled different from my Mum who always wore a scent called Californian Poppy. Their smell was a combination of lavender and mothballs.

But back to the tea. At last it would be time to go through to the best room and sit down, and plates and dishes were handed round with the invitation to take as much as we wanted. The ham was sliced by hand, much thicker than I was used to. Our boiled ham which appeared when we had visitors for tea, used to be bought at the corner shop, Mr Surr's, and was cut thinly on his huge bacon slicer. Here, at the aunties', it was chewy and pink and didn't go down all in one mouthful. To accompany the ham there was tongue, meat that I hardly ever saw elsewhere other than in the pork butcher's window. The accompanying salad in this house meant not just a lettuce leaf, a slice of tomato, and a slice of cucumber, as it did at home, but dishes of fresh homegrown produce.

On our summer visit there, (we came just twice a year) tea was always memorable for the tour of the garden which prefaced it, when we picked a big tender lettuce from the soil, and chose ripe red tomatoes from the tall plants in their greenhouse. I was allowed to pull fat, red radishes from the ground where they were growing in their neat rows. I think cucumbers were probably bought in as I don't remember the aunties growing these, but they were avid gardeners. That summer tea was always followed by a long walk down the leafy lanes nearby when I would return with an armful of wild flowers. No one stopped us picking wild flowers in those days.

However, this was the Christmas tea, so the slices of ham and tongue were accompanied by dishes of home made pickles. In the pantry we had already been shown this year's garden harvest – shelves of pickled brown onions in malt vinegar, bright red cabbage and my favourite, piccalilli. I was fascinated by its deep yellow mustardy colour and always went straight for that dish, hoping to find a sauce-covered piece of pickled cauliflower. For some reason the fact that cauliflower could be pickled rather than boiled lifeless, always fascinated me. My Dad sometimes had a go at pickling onions before Christmas and they would sit in their jars under the sink in the kitchen, in the dark, until they were ready, but I had never known anyone before who could make piccalilli. To go alongside all this were plates of homemade bread, buttered not too sparingly. Looking back, some of these early years that I remember must have been in years of food rationing when the butter allowance was just two ounces a week, but there never seemed to be a shortage of food on their table. When the plates had been cleared from the ham course, then came the "afters". At home we always offered visitors tinned peaches with Carnation milk. That was the norm. It never varied. Here we had a choice of tinned fruit, trifle, or my favourite – tinned pears set in a dish of red jelly. To go with it was real cream poured out of a jug. No wonder I loved being there for tea.

Finally we reached the point when the nearby sideboard, which had been covered with an embroidered tablecloth, was uncovered to reveal a festival of cakes. The aunts were nothing if they were not bakers supreme. It seemed to me that I was gazing into a cake shop window with the number and variety that they produced. First the classic Victoria Sponge, set on its glass cake-stand, lightly sprinkled with sugar, neighboured by chocolate éclairs that were made for my Mum, as they were her favourite. For my father, his favourite seed cake – he always had a slice at teatime and then was given the rest to take home. At first I never knew what the seeds were, and even later I never heard anyone mention caraway seeds outside that house. There were maids of honour (little tarts with a ground almond filling over raspberry jam), currant slices and jam tarts, on a three-tiered cake-stand, and then in mid-sideboard, my special choice, a wonderful chocolate cake that not only tasted dark and rich but also had chocolate butter icing gluing the two sponge halves together. When I think of that sideboard spread now, it was no wonder that the aunties were well-rounded. Perhaps a couple of slices from each cake-plate were eaten at teatime, and then presumably they would eat their way through the remainder in the following days. Never short on calories in that house, I imagine.

It was all such a treat and such a contrast to the way we usually ate at home. My father was a storekeeper in a large engineering works in Beeston – Forgrove Machinery Company – and as such didn't bring home a big wage. My mum did eventually go to work too when I was judged old enough to leave for that hour between me finishing school and her finishing work, but in the early years they must have struggled on one meagre wage and there was not a lot in the way of food. The aunties on the other hand were quite well off, the only branch of my father's family with any money. Living on the outskirts of the city, they had access to friends with smallholdings providing extra eggs and dairy food. These were the post-war years when rationing was still very much in evidence for the majority. Auntie Nellie had been married to a self-employed builder, who had built the pair of bungalows where they lived, as well as many of the surrounding bungalows and houses. They were not wealthy in today's sense of the word but did have a different way of life from our own. Neither of the ladies had ever had any need to work outside the home to augment their income so they did have the time to knit, sew, do needlework and tend the garden, all hobbies which mapped out a different homelife from the one where I was brought up. Mum did have a go with a needle, mainly to alter the dresses for me that were passed on from an older cousin, but I never saw her knit or take up a piece of decorative stitching. My mum spent her spare time playing cards, and was good enough to be regularly in the prizewinners at local whist-drives that she and my father attended twice a week.

I somehow knew that the aunties were richer than us, because of the abundance of everything at their house compared to our more basic standard of living at home. They lived in bungalows whereas where we lived there were no bungalows, only street after street of back-to-back terrace houses. And I knew that my parents paid rent but heard them talking of the aunties owning their houses. Our living room (and by that I mean the one room where we lived as opposed to the two bedrooms or the little cellar kitchen) had a three-piece suite, well worn and lumpy, a sideboard, a table and four straight backed chairs where we ate our meals, and much later, a TV in the corner. In the aunties' house there were two living rooms, one with comfortable sofas and a couple of upholstered chairs all with comfy cushions and crocheted back covers. The window ledges had cut-glass vases and nice china ornaments, while the only ornaments in our house were a polished mantle clock that belonged to my father and a plaster figure known as the whistling boy that stood on the sideboard. The other room, their best room, had a long dining table and six chairs around it and a large dresser as well as a sideboard along one side. My mum always referred to their furniture as big ugly old stuff but I imagine that these pieces of solid furniture were probably another indication of the difference between our worlds.

Moving on from furniture to compare the differences in what our two families ate, I had seen vegetables and salad being grown before as my father had an allotment near to our house where he grew potatoes and cabbages, onions and carrots. I imagine this was a result of the national wartime drive to grow your own food. But I don't remember having homegrown salad at all and it certainly would not have been tomatoes or cucumbers, as we didn't have a greenhouse. So these visits to the aunties were really my first glimpse of what living "the good life" could be like. I'm sure that it was there that the seeds were sown for my love of good food.

2

Grandma's Baking Days

Grandma's Recipe for Jam Sponge

2 eggs
2 oz butter
½ cup fine sugar
small cup flour
½ teasp baking powder

Bake in a moderate oven

This is all she has written in her recipe book

Translate fine sugar as caster sugar (2 oz)

Flour would have been plain flour (4 oz)

And eggs would probably be medium rather than large.

I would bake this at gas mark 5 for about 20 minutes.

By the time I was nine years old my world had expanded somewhat and I had gradually learned many important facts. The first was that I had realised that I was a clever girl, so much so that I had been lifted out of my year group at school and placed in the year higher, which also meant I had left all my friends behind. The new teacher, Miss Brown, was reputed to be a real tartar but I found her strict but fair and I revelled in the work that she designed specially for me. When my mother was taken into hospital suffering from a duodenal ulcer Miss Brown was so thoughtful, sending me straight back home one morning with flowers and magazines. Having left my friends from the class below, I now felt a bit lonely in my hours at school but it didn't deter my thirst for learning. I remember my Mum saying things like "I wonder where she gets it from?" referring to my ability at school. It was about this time that I found out why she said these words – the second major realisation in my life.

As I remember it, on this particular day we had been talking in the school playground at break-time and I had been listening to a conversation about a girl who was the daughter of our local greengrocer. The talk was that this girl had been "adopted" – a word I had never heard before and didn't really understand. At four o'clock

I trotted home and after tea I remembered about the playground conversation and announced that I had heard that the greengrocer's daughter was adopted, adding, "Am I adopted?" There was a silence and I remember Mum answering, "Well would it matter if you were?" to which I said, " No I don't think so". Then the whole story came out. Apparently my parents had adopted me at six weeks old, as they seemed to be unable to have a child of their own. From that day on, my mother always believed that someone who knew about my adoption had whispered in my ear, but nothing like that happened. It was pure coincidence that I overheard the playground conversation and followed it up with a question. At the time I was totally unaffected by the news. But later in my life it had other repercussions.

By this age, I had also been trusted to walk to my Grandma's house alone, a distance of about a mile and a half. Sadly, very different from the leeway we can allow children today. Grandma had been widowed many years before, and had always lived in an end terrace house in Holbeck. It had a main room and kitchen downstairs, with two small bedrooms above. The kitchen was where Monday washday happened centred around the huge wringing machine, and if I was there during school holidays I was allowed to turn the handle while she fed through the folded linen. I found it all strangely exciting with the steamy piles of laundry; with that peculiar smell they have as they are pulled from the boiler, and the sink full of dolly-blue rinse for the white cloths.

The main room was where the rest of life happened. Probably ironing followed on Tuesday. Was Wednesday the day for polishing the ornaments and windows? I can't really remember that but I know Thursday was her baking day. For such a small room there was an abundance of furniture. A large curved-front, five-drawer cabinet stood in one corner polished to a remarkable sheen. There was a huge high-backed sideboard along another wall flanked on each side by great big Victorian pictures, one of which was Monarch of the Glen. A piano filled the wall between the door and the bedroom staircase, and as well as four heavy upholstered dining chairs and a horse-hair stuffed rocking chair, there was an enormous dining table in the centre of the room which for six days of the week was dressed in a thick caramel-brown plush table cloth with a fruit bowl in the middle.

However, every Thursday the cloth came off to reveal a scrubbed oak table ready to support the day's baking. Linen bags of flour came out of the kitchen cupboard and as bread was the first item on the list, a huge, straight-sided, brown earthenware bowl with a thick cream rim was lifted out and the flour, foaming yeast liquid and a handful of salt were poured in then mixed together until they were ready to pummel on the floured table top. I think I learned to knead bread at this early age simply by watching Grandma push and turn the dough time after time until she was happy that it was just right to be left to rise on the hearth. The first rising was always done in that huge bowl covered by a wet tea-towel, then came a second shorter pummelling, after which the dough was cut up into several pieces and each piece shaped into a round, and placed into tins for the final rise before baking. While this kneading went on the fire was stoked continually to bring up the heat of the oven in the black range, and it reached exactly the right temperature just as the dough was ready. When the loaves came out of the oven they were fat brown cobs ready for a quick brush over with milk, then popped back for two minutes and finally emerging shiny where the milk had changed into a brown glaze.

After bread Grandma baked teacakes in roughly the same way but using sweetened milk in the mix, and into half the mixture, adding currants. Then it was on to my favourite item on the baking list – pastry. In those days nobody talked of cholesterol, good and bad fats, or being overweight. In the post-war years we were still eating frugally, walking everywhere and very few people could be described as overweight. Consequently everyone who made pastry used lard, or possibly the newer margarine that was on the market, but lard produced the best results in terms of light flakiness. A huge amount of pastry was mixed up, one or two pies were made, followed by jam tarts and finally, to finish, my own favourite, jam pasty. For this all the remaining pastry was rolled out flat with grandma's big rolling pin, half of it was spread with strawberry or raspberry jam, then the rest of it was folded over the jammed half and all the edges sealed together so that jam couldn't escape. The trick was to slide this large unwieldy piece of unbaked pastry onto a baking sheet without any damage, before brushing the top with milk and popping it into the top shelf of the oven. When it came out it was cut up into pieces about the size of a small chocolate bar, and to my great pleasure there were always one or two breakages that were passed to me. I wonder whether the breakages were deliberate?

Grandma continued to have her regular weekly baking day until she was almost eighty when her eyesight failed due to cataracts. Then I took over the shopping for her and we found the best quality bread came from Knapton's bakery a few streets away. The bread order was always the same – a small white loaf and four currant teacakes.

The teacakes were usually warm and smelled wonderful, but my weakness was the four crusty bottom corners of the white loaf which I nibbled while walking home. I was always scolded severely but it never stopped me doing it the next time.

3

Sunday Mornings

Mum's recipe for Savoury Pudding

This is a handed-down recipe from Grandma, and Mum would sometimes serve this before the main course as an alternative to Yorkshire Pudding

2–3 large onions sliced and chopped
½ loaf of stale bread soaked in milk or water then chopped up
Dessertspoon plain flour or fine oatmeal to bind
Salt & pepper
2 teasp dried sage
1 medium egg
dripping or oil for baking tin

Put tin with dripping or oil in oven to heat (gas mark 6-7)

Mix all ingredients together thoroughly – mixture should be rough and lumpy rather than too smooth.

Pour into heated baking tin and bake for 45 minutes until golden brown on top.

Serve with onion gravy.

My Sundays always followed the same pattern. I would get up with Mum and Dad about half eight or nine o'clock, eat my breakfast – on Sundays, usually one rasher of fried bacon with a piece of white sliced bread – and then get ready for Sunday School. My parents were not churchgoers at all but from the age of three I had gone along to the Methodist Church at the end of the road in the company of a family who lived further down the street, the Storeys. When I think about it now, very few people do that any more, but then everyone seemed to encourage their children to go to Sunday School, even though they would never think of going there themselves. Perhaps they saw it as doing their bit towards giving children a religious education, or perhaps it was simply a good way to get rid of the kids for an hour or so, once or even twice on Sundays.

The Methodist Chapel in Dewsbury Road is no longer there. It was pulled down in the late sixties to make way for a new commercial building. Presumably that site was valuable being on the main road, but it was such a shame to destroy such a beautiful building. It's one of my early memories – being awed by its beauty and the craftsmanship. The building was tiered with a gallery right round it, and the whole interior gleamed with polished golden oak. Every pew held probably six people and the wooden seat was made a little more comfortable with a red plush runner along it to sit down on. There was a pulpit across the front, and behind the pulpit sat the choir at the far end of the gallery. In my teens I joined the choir and remember singing my first solo, "Hear My Prayer" generally recognised as "Oh for the Wings of a Dove", from that gallery.

From being very young, I was quite happy to go to Sunday School, as I enjoyed everything that happened there. In the morning session we went into church first and sang alongside the adults, then just before the minister started on his sermon, we left, and went into an assortment of small rooms to listen to a bible story, colour in a drawing of the story, or do some other activity, according to the age you'd reached. Sunday School started at half past ten, and the service ended around a quarter to twelve, and I would always run to the front entrance where my father would be waiting for me to take our weekly walk.

Looking back at the relationships we had as a family when I was a child, I know that these Sunday mornings were what he thought of as his contribution to bringing me up. Mum and Dad had adopted me when I was six weeks old after trying for a child unsuccessfully for five years. They both married late so there was not too much time left to go on trying. During the war there were lots of children up for adoption so I imagine they didn't have to wait very long to get me. Dad used to tell me that he pushed me in my pushchair from being a toddler, first over Woodhouse Ridge when they lived in Glossop Mount, and later up to Cross Flatts Park when they moved to Dewsbury Road. Years later he was to repeat exactly the same trips for my children in their pushchairs, in spite of being well over seventy years old.

Our walks were always on a Sunday morning, as that was the only day he didn't work. At that time he had a job in an engineering factory and Saturday morning overtime was compulsory and welcome, because of the extra bit of money it brought in. As I got to the age where I could walk with him, the pushchair was discarded, and by the time I was about nine or ten we were doing regular four or five mile Sunday morning walks. I can't remember what we talked about or whether we walked hand in hand, but I think we both looked forward to them. Certainly until I became a moody teenager, I never thought of not going with him.

We would set off from the church at the end of Burton Road, straight up Dewsbury Road until we were clear of the parade of shops and the Crescent cinema, then veer off left behind the cinema and within two minutes already be into fields and hedgerows. From there we tramped past the Rugby League ground where Hunslet played and within a couple of minutes we were in the edges of Middleton Woods, climbing up alongside the tram track until we reached a huge open space on top of the hill which we knew as Middleton Clearings. Many years later when my father died, mum having died the previous year, I chose to scatter his ashes on Middleton Clearings, as it was there that we spent so many hours together. Both amateur soccer and rugby teams played matches up here on Sundays and we would stand for a while watching them and then Dad would always say, "Well we'd better be off or we won't be back in time for the Yorkshire Puddings".

Half past one was the absolute deadline for Sunday lunch, so we would walk back home then, going a slightly different way back with me picking wild flowers, bluebells or buttercups according to the time of the year, so that I could plant them in a milk bottle on the outside window ledge near the cellar kitchen. There were never any rules about not picking bluebells then, and in fact on Monday mornings at school there were lots of bunches lined up in milk bottles on the classroom window sills, showing that many children had the same Sunday walk habit as we did.

After washing my hands, I sat down at the table for lunch (or Sunday dinner as we called it then) and watched my Mum, usually red-faced and hot by this time, as she lifted out the first batch of Yorkshire puddings from the oven. Yorkshire Pudding was one of her culinary triumphs, whether they were medium sized ones done in Victoria sponge tins, or little puddings cooked in bun-tins. These little marvels would rise to a good four or five inches and were crisp and golden but still slightly soft on the inside. I remember being given a whole large crispy brown pudding for my first course (the traditional Yorkshire way is to eat puddings before the main roast course – presumably to fill you up so that you wouldn't need so much meat) and although my parents would pour rich onion gravy over theirs, my pudding usually was covered with squeezed orange juice and a bit of sugar.

Then on to the main course which in spite of us not having much money to go round, was always a roast joint. Sometimes this was half a leg of lamb served with mint sauce made with fresh mint from the little patch of a garden out front. Sometimes it was a bit of brisket of beef, a rolled joint that had a bit more fat on it than I preferred, but tasty all the same. I also clearly recall on occasions having roast veal – a strange shoulder cut that seemed very bubbly with pale pink flesh before it was cooked. I had no idea at the time what veal was and which animal it came from. We usually would have roast potatoes with beef or veal but with lamb we had new potatoes if possible, sometimes pulled fresh from my Dad's allotment. However the thing which spoiled the meal for me was the green veg bit. My mum had always cooked anything green with bicarbonate of soda – a handy hint from her Mum to keep the colour of green vegetables. But it was the fashion then that they were cooked for ages, often half an hour or more, and chopped up to look like a puree. Chopping the cauliflower in our cracked yellow pudding basin was always my job, and I disliked the taste of the end result so very much. No taste of cauliflower just a strong taste of bicarb accompanying a mushy, watery, green mess, as of course some of the outer leaves of the cauliflower were cooked too, as well as the white flower!

We usually had a pudding – apple sponge was my Mum's usual offering as she could whip this one up very quickly without too much trouble. It was cooked in a small enamel pie dish that in later years served as a dog bowl if I remember rightly. I don't recall having custard with that pudding, instead Mum would pour over the sweetened juice from stewing the apples. If in the event we had no sweet pudding to follow, then another batch of Yorkshires would be produced and this time everyone had orange juice and sugar and ate them as afters.

Dad and I would have arrived home from our long walk at about one-thirty, and lunch was on the table in a flash. We all gathered round the table sitting in the downstairs cellar-kitchen, and I wolfed down three courses, quickly washed my face and hands, and ran back up the road for session two at Sunday School which started at two o'clock. I firmly believe that this was how I came to be a bolter of food. To this day I can clear my plate faster than anyone I know. I also realise that it's not good for me, and I've tried to slow myself down, but those Sunday School sessions have a lot to answer for.

4

School
Dinners

Recipe for Manchester Tart

This is a simple compilation of a pastry case (either bought or made with 6 oz flour and 3 oz margarine), first spread with raspberry or strawberry jam, then filled with custard which is made from a pint of milk and three tablespoons of custard powder. Allow the custard to cool and set firm. Some versions then sprinkle on coconut or simply decorate with glace cherries. Occasionally you may find a version with sliced bananas under the custard instead of, or as well as, the jam.

Mention school dinners and most people will pull faces and tell tales of horrible meals fit only for the pigswill bucket. For me the school dinner experience was exactly the opposite, an introduction to all manner of exciting, different things to eat and different ways of serving food, that left lasting good memories. Whoever was in charge of our school canteen certainly knew how to cook and we were never given anything but good wholesome food.

I had left my junior school, Hunslet Moor Primary School, after passing my eleven plus examination and had opted to attend the nearby co-educational grammar school that was Cockburn High School. On Burton Road, it was a two-minute walk from where we lived, and as far as I could see, the only thing against it was the brown and yellow uniform. There was a brown woollen blazer, a belted gabardine raincoat worn with a brown beret of course, and to crown it all, even my knickers had to be regulation mud brown. It's taken me fifty years to get over the trauma of wearing brown, but suddenly over the last few years it is now a fashionable colour, smart enough to replace the classic black, and so I have overcome my long-lived distaste. On the whole looking back at five long years at Grammar School does not fill me with horror. I was learning and discovering a new world and the biggest shock was to find that there were other children as clever as I was. At primary school I had always been top of the class even after it was decided that I should move up a year around the age of nine. Every lesson just seemed to come easily without any effort. At Cockburn I found myself in the "A" stream, and always in the top handful, but never quite in that easy position way out in front of everyone else, and having to try really hard to be first in any exam subject was something quite new for me, and didn't do me any harm at all, I'm sure. In fact I realise that I'm still quite competitive and still aim to be the best at anything I tackle.

In those five years I learned that I could shine in Latin, mainly because I gained the knack of turning my translation efforts into something that resembled a real story, rather than lots of phrases tacked together without any real meaning. I usually had to read out my translation for Miss Milner (always dressed in tailored suits) and the rest of the class. And biology lessons opened my eyes to the wonders of the world, and that love of nature and all things botanical has stayed with me. I particularly loved the study of plants even though my drawings were a bit heavy-handed and ugly. On the other hand chemistry and physics were subjects I never seemed to understand and it still remains a mystery to me how aeroplanes stay in the air and how electricity is produced.

And it was at Cockburn High School that I discovered I had a singing voice. In the final two years of school we were allowed to audition for the end of year drama production; one year would see a classic play, and in the alternate year there would be a Gilbert and Sullivan production. I went to audition for "Pirates of Penzance". There were a couple of girls who were known to have singing lessons, the blonde and beautiful Kathleen Lunn, and another girl in her class, Pauline Thomas. The audition piece was "Poor Wandering One" the soprano solo with rather high final notes. The front runners did their auditions and then all the rest of us who had turned up sang in pairs the first time through to get to know the tune, then repeated the song as a solo. I could feel my stomach heaving with butterflies when it was my turn, and I sang the duet first with my friend from church, Hilda, and then suddenly I was on my own. I remember that it was like hearing another voice singing rather than mine, as this stronger, better noise came out of my mouth almost unbidden. Everyone seemed really surprised and no-one more so than me. The music teacher, Mr Eades, asked how long I had been singing like that and I had to reply that it was the first time I had heard that voice myself. Unfortunately as regards the school production, I was later taken on one side and told that in spite of my newly discovered lovely voice, I would not have any main part because I was far too tall. I had grown to be five foot ten inches by the time I was thirteen, and of course all the boys in the same year who would have played opposite me were a good six inches shorter at least, so it was a no-go. It was one of my first real lessons in unfairness and disappointment. However the discovery of my voice was to bring me great pleasure all through my life and I have never lost the joy of singing.

My Mum had started to work full-time at a nearby clothing factory by this time, so I was now a candidate for school dinners, as she wouldn't think of letting me come home at lunchtime and fend for myself – no-one did that then. Our morning lessons ended at 12.25, and after the bell had gone we marched down the street in a crocodile and over the little road into the dinner huts which I remember as a series of pre-fabricated buildings that were rather badly lit inside, but each one a hive of activity. The yellow gingham covered tables all seated either eight children, four sitting down each side on wooden benches, or every other table would have seven pupils and a teacher at the head of the table. Never more than eight in total as all the dishes, be it a pot full of stew or a large round flan, divided into eight good portions but no more. Each table had a server who had to queue by the serving hatches down one end of the canteen and take loaded trays over to his or her table. Then either the teacher or the server gave out the food. We could usually smell what it was when came through the outer doors, especially when it was beef stew, or fish on Fridays.

I must try to avoid making my mum sound like a rotten cook, as she wasn't, it was more that she cooked everything in the way her mother had taught her, and that was to boil everything to death as was then the fashion; and there was a limited number of variations on the menus we had each day. As I said before, at home when Mum cooked vegetables – cabbage, cauliflower, savoy or even green peas – she always added bicarbonate of soda "to keep it green". It was what she had been taught to do and I think many other housewives used the same rule. Unfortunately the result was a dish of mushed green vegetable rather like a soggy puree, well before purees became a fashionable item on any menu. Here in the school canteen each casserole dish of vegetables held cabbage or carrots that had been cooked but not done to death, and actually tasted of the veg itself instead of tasting the bitter bicarb. Then the potatoes – ah the potatoes! Mashed potatoes were mashed with butter (or perhaps it was margarine), and roast potatoes were so crisp and crunchy. Again it was all very different from my food experience at home.

One of the most memorable tastes was their beef casserole, which came in a pale green, lidded dish full to the brim with good sized chunks of tender meat and thick dark gravy. This was the dish that, while I loved the overall taste of the meat, I had a small difficulty with the fat. I had developed an early aversion to fatty meat of any kind and if I drew a chunk of beef that proved to have a good piece of yellow fat attached to it, I was horrified, as we were not allowed to take anything from our mouths once it was inside. I did deal with it by taking my courage and swallowing it down, but I shuddered. In the range of main courses beef casserole was the stunner, but we regularly had roast lamb, beef or pork all carved into good thick slices arranged on their serving dishes and accompanied by jugs of "proper gravy". As I mentioned, it was usually fish on Friday and often cooked almost as we bought it from the fish shop, battered, and it came with chips – one of the few times we were served chips at all. The other dish that did come with chips, was in summer, when a serving platter of cold sliced ham would be accompanied with lots of fresh salad and a portion of nice fat brown chips.

As I moved further up the school I progressed to being a server myself and at times I recall also being on duty to help in setting the tables and getting everything ready for the meal. The lady in charge of the canteen was a Mrs Miller, a short rounded bustling woman, who marshalled her brigade in a smiling but firm manner, and she always had us running round setting gleaming knives and forks across all the tables. Perhaps that's where I learned the right way to place a spoon and fork above the plate. Being a server really came into its own on the pudding course – and what a wonderful variety of puddings we enjoyed. Everyone moans about school tapioca and sago pudding but I can hold my hand on my heart and say I honestly loved them, indeed I loved all the range of milk puddings – rice, sago, tapioca and semolina, all creamy and thick and served with a jug of pouring fruit syrup or hot jam – mmmm! Then there were the fruit flans. One of the most remarkable looking – and tasting – was the blackcurrant fruit base with an unusual lilac/pink topping of a sort of marshmallow over it. Perhaps it sounds yucky and garish but it was heaven and exactly the colour and taste that children love. Flans also might be filled with strawberries and glazed over with thickened strawberry juice – a lovely summer version, or with tinned apricots and again glazed to look sumptuous and glistening.

I read in a magazine recently that a reader was remembering Manchester Tart from her schooldays and asking whether anyone had a recipe. It was also a speciality on our school meal menu and as I recall its pastry base was first covered in strawberry jam then thick custard and allowed to set. Sometimes there was the addition of grated coconut on top. And speaking of custard why can I never make custard like I remember school custard. Ours was a pale yellow and so thick and creamy. Perhaps the secret was that it was made with sterilised milk that was then so freely available. And from my memories of flans and tarts we move to sponge puddings. These came either in the form of a tray-bake slab cake, perhaps a sponge layer covered with jam and then coconut, and served of course with custard, or perhaps as a fruit bottomed sponge – apples or rhubarb – in a deep casserole dish. Moving swiftly on to traditional steamed puddings, here I can happily admit that my mum made a very good steamed ginger sponge from time to time, so I was already schooled in the art of producing a good steamed pudding, but again school dinners had its own little triumph. The very best in their sponge range was steamed chocolate pudding served with chocolate custard. Absolute decadence!

There are also vivid memories of equally vivid pink blancmange that was served with jelly and large homemade biscuits. And Christmas was wonderful when after the mountains of sprouts had been eaten (and they were well cooked sprouts at least) a huge steamed Christmas pudding would be placed on each table with the usual jug of custard replaced by a jug of nutmeg-spiced white sauce. I had never seen sweet white sauce before eating those school dinners, and the pudding had real sixpences in – whatever would Health and Safety say today?

Until I started to write down my school dinner food list I had no idea that they had made such an impression on me. Certainly any child who ate in our school canteen would have been well nourished and never hungry. Thinking of those days has created a warm glow of a memory. Excuse me while I go and try to make a rice pudding that compares with my school dinner memories!

5

Leaving
for Italy

Rabbit and Chicken a la Signora Belgrano

1 rabbit – good quality – ask the
butcher to cut it into 6 pieces
6 chicken thighs
12 slices of thinly cut prosciutto
ham (or back bacon)
1 teasp dried oregano
salt & pepper
olive oil

Wrap each piece of rabbit or
chicken with prosciutto

Place pieces in a large roasting
tin – not too close together.

Dribble olive oil over everything
and make sure all pieces are
oil-covered. Sprinkle oregano,
salt and pepper.

Cook in moderately hot oven
Gas mark 6 for 45–60 minutes
until cooked.

Having a love affair is exciting enough, but experiencing the anticipation before embarking on a love affair, can be even more thrilling. This is exactly how I was feeling, having said my goodbyes to my tearful parents; I stepped on the train at Leeds City Station, the train that was to take me overland to Italy on my big adventure.

I was 19. My friend Pat Little, who had grown up with me as we lived on the opposite sides of the street in Longroyd Place, (I at No4 and Pat at No3) had three months previously answered an advertisement in The Lady magazine and as a result had left her job in the offices of Hunslet Engine Co. and had gone off to be an *au pair* girl living-in with an Italian family in Genoa (or Genova as we came to use its Italian name). Her letters home had painted a new and different outlook on life, a life that seemed exciting and full of the unknown, so much so that I had horrified my parents by asking her to look out for a post for me, so that I too could turn my back on British office life and head for Italy. At 16 I had achieved a coveted place in the Civil Service (a steady job for life!), working in the Ministry of Labour, and after three and a half years was supposedly "doing well". You can understand why my parents were so worried and mystified as to why I wanted to do this. People didn't do things like "taking a year out to travel" in those days, or perhaps more particularly didn't do things like that where we came from, south of the River Aire in Leeds.

I think also their feelings were bound up with having adopted me, and somehow feeling that I should be forever indebted to them for that act. How could I therefore be thinking of going away and leaving them? This feeling that they expected me to be forever grateful and pay them back in kind, cropped up as long as my mother lived, and was to become a deep hurt that eventually prevented me from any strong feelings of love towards her. Her often-repeated sentences when we were at loggerheads with one another were "I thought you'd have been grateful to us, after all we've done for you. We took you so that you could look after us in our old age". She probably never realised the enormity of these words and how they made me feel, and I'm sure there was a better, more worthy reason to adopt me, but she never moved from that mind-set and regrettably it caused many arguments between us in the years before she died.

So Pat had written back to my request with an immediate "Yes, come and join me. There are dozens of families looking for English girls here", and without any hesitation on my part, my month's notice was given at the office, horrifying my bosses too I might add, and so here I was on the platform of Leeds City Station, waving goodbye to my mother and father. I had the details of the family I was to go to, by all accounts a very rich family who wanted someone to speak English to their younger son. The first leg of my journey was to take me to London, where I would join the boat train at Victoria Station which linked with the ferry from Dover to Calais. Then having boarded the train again I was to be carried across

Europe via France and Switzerland, and eventually into Italy arriving at midday in Milan Station where Pat should be waiting.

This was my first time abroad, and I tried to contain the excitement that if I am honest was combined with elements of doubt and worry about doing the right thing, as I sat for the first part of my journey after Calais, totally alone in the carriage. By early evening, the time we were weaving through the outskirts of Paris, an attendant had visited the carriage where I was seated and had turned down the seats and transformed them into sleeping couchettes for the night. I decided that the journey would pass more quickly if I lay down and tried to sleep. Being alone in the carriage, I undressed, slipped on my nightdress, bought new for the trip, and climbed into my narrow and somewhat uncomfortable bed.

I had been dozing for about an hour when the train slowed to a stop. I had no idea where we were and I was horrified to realise that another passenger, a man, had been shown into my carriage and seeing me asleep, or pretending to be so, was trying to get into his bunk with as little noise as possible. Through my half closed eyelids I watched the trousered legs moving up and down, worrying what might come next. Then I saw that he simply slipped off his shoes and lay down without removing his clothes. I thanked God for that but immediately realised that at some point I had to dress in his presence the next morning. With this worry on my mind I drifted in and out of sleep for a few hours until about six or seven o'clock the next day, and woke up realising that my fellow passenger was preparing to leave our compartment, presumably to visit the small washroom at the end of the carriage for his morning ablutions. I grabbed the chance and shot out from under my blanket, threw on my clothes from the night before, and by the time he returned after five minutes or so I was sitting bolt upright, on my bed, fully dressed and composed on the surface, as if I did this all the time. "Bonjour Monsieur" I offered in my "I've passed my GCE" French, and he smiled while looking somewhat puzzled. My first ever continental breakfast of a small piece of baguette and a croissant, was brought in by the carriage service and my companion and I ate together. It seemed to me somewhat light as a breakfast, but one I would come to enjoy. We chatted in French in a stilted fashion over the next hour, and then he gathered his things together, politely wished me good luck, and got off somewhere beyond the Swiss border, whereupon I heaved a huge sigh of relief.

I was due into Milan station just before midday, so in the last hour I gathered my things together and sat with my old-fashioned and somewhat battered brown leather suitcase primed and ready, feeling my excitement building. As the train pulled onto the platform I could already see Pat scanning the carriage windows looking for me. I clambered down from the dizzy heights of the high continental train with my luggage and ran to meet her. After exchanging hugs and gifts (I had brought out some things for her from her parents), she took me by the arm and led me off towards the outside of the station. A celebratory lunch was called for, and having eaten my first early morning continental breakfast on the train, my stomach was now rumbling. This was no ordinary lunch for me. It was my very first taste of Italian food, and it was to begin a love affair with Mediterranean cuisine that would last me a lifetime. In England, I had never eaten pasta, indeed we had just suffered the humiliation of the April Fools Day scam of seeing the "spaghetti crop" being gathered from trees in Italy, broadcast on our screens in a Panorama programme. The words "pizza and pasta" were new in my vocabulary.

Pat had brought me to what I remember now as a sort of takeaway establishment selling fresh-baked pizza straight from the wood oven, rather like the food outlets we now see at our own railway stations. But the wood oven made the difference. Now, seasoned travellers to Italy will confirm that pizza in Italy is nothing like the pizzas which are now on sale all over Britain. Real Italian pizzas are light and thin crusted, with so many fresh flavours from the toppings that they are a gourmet delight. Seated at a small table on the outer limits of the architecturally beautiful Milan railway station, with its high Art Deco arches resembling Grand Central Station, New York, I sampled my first pizza, and fell in love. It was made from ingredients that were all new to me – fresh tomatoes with real flavour, melted stretching pieces of mozzarella cheese, herbs and olive oil! It was the stunning combination that made me sit up. With that in my stomach I could face meeting my Italian family for the first time. Little did I know that this first meeting was to turn into a bit of an ordeal.

Having eaten our fill, Pat and I boarded another train for the last part of the journey, which would take me to Genova. When we arrived there she guided me towards a grey-uniformed chauffeur who was standing by a large gleaming car. Signora Fasce, my new employer, was sitting in the back of the car and she eventually slid out of the car door to greet me, and she laughed openly at some private joke with her chauffeur, making me feel a little uncomfortable. The family, other than Paulo, the young school-boy I was to coach, spoke no English, so I understood not a word. After a few minutes conversation between Signora Fasce and Pat, who was already doing very well with the Italian language, I was encouraged to get into the car with her and I waved goodbye to Pat as we drew away. There followed a shopping expedition, with the Signora stopping the car every so often, sending out the chauffeur on various errands, then off again. This was punctuated with Italian conversation directed at me, to which I could only smile helplessly.

We reached the house about an hour later and more formal introductions followed with the house staff (again more laughter at some private joke) and an old —nay very, very old — grandma, who was given the task of showing me over the twenty-six rooms of the house. So for the next hour I was taken round, at snail's pace, being shown pictures of ancestors etc. with a fixed smile on my face, understanding nothing and wondering why on earth I had made the decision to come to this quite unwelcoming household. Perhaps there was also a little bit of homesickness creeping in too. But the tour was over eventually and I was shown to a small room in the servants' quarters and by pointing at the hands on the clock, I learned that I was to go back in an hour for dinner. It seemed that at least I was to eat with the family. As we sat down there was more discussion in my direction and it was eventually explained to me when my young nine year old charge arrived, and was able to translate for me, that they had misunderstood from my letter that I was very small, presumably they read "very small" for "very tall". I am actually five foot ten inches tall so when I arrived at the station and they saw me they wondered what all other English girls looked like if I was a sample of "small". Hence the tittering!

That little matter cleared up, we sat down to dinner and I learned more about Italian cuisine as served in a rather well-to-do Northern Italian household. First course – *minestra* i.e. small pasta in broth, second course some type of meat or fish, with vegetables served as a separate course, followed by fresh fruit. I honestly cannot remember exactly what we ate that night as I was so overawed by the experience, and the opulence of the dining room, but I soon learned over the next weeks that the format was the same each night. I do recall having what we came to know as a "fish week" once every so often, when I would accompany the Signora down the Ligurian coast to Camogli, a small fishing village, where she would buy every variety of fresh fish imaginable from the boats at the quayside, and there followed every night until it ran out, fish, fish, fish. One of these fishy evenings produced my first meeting with whitebait, not deep fried as I later found was more common, but poached in a herby broth which produced a huge pile of what looked like small white worms all with their eyes firmly staring at me. These days I would still have had a go, but in my inexperienced state, I declined the offer of tasting that one!

My job with the Fasce family lasted only a matter of weeks, as I found they were not a very hospitable family to live with, plus their older son had amorous designs on me that were very unwelcome. Looking back it was probably that they saw my post as that of a servant whereas in Pat's household she was treated as one of the family, which is how living as an *au pair* should be. However I was fortunate enough to be introduced to the Durand family who were looking for a live-in help and when I joined them I knew family life here would be very different. They were nowhere near as rich as the Fasce family, in fact they lived in an apartment in the not very fashionable end of Genova, but they were very good people and we are still in touch today. I looked after two small girls, Miriam and Patrizia, aged three and eighteen months, and there was another baby on the way. Life was one long round of chores and cooking but I learned so much about real Italian family life, and of course lots about the Italian table. I would go to shop at the market, and before I left the flat I was directed by Signora Durand as to which cheese to buy, how to look at vegetables and know which were best, and I became an accomplished cook at the simpler Italian dishes. I also had my first confrontation with a suppository that I was handed to administer to Miriam when she had a cough. I totally misunderstood what it was and was quite appalled when it was eventually explained what I had to do with it, but I learned that this was the preferable way to take medication in Italy!

Each week I had a day off which I usually spent with Pat and the other English girlfriends also working for Italian families in Genova. During the summer Pat went off with her family to their house on the Riviera, and I arranged to see her on one of my days off. Pat and I met in Portofino in the morning and we gathered together wine and cheese and bread for a picnic. I made everyone in the shop laugh by asking for 200 grams of Fontana instead of Fontina, the difference being that one is a variety of cheese and the other is a fountain! We trekked up the hill and found a place to sit outside the house we were told belonged to Rex Harrison and I recall that we thought we were in the best place in the world as we sat there outside of a famous film star's house, drinking red wine and eating a simple picnic with gourmet ingredients. We talked about things we remembered from our childhood but after a while the effect of the sun or the wine, or probably the combination of the two, was too much, and we collapsed in giggles.

On another day off, I was invited for a meal with Pat's family, the Belgranos, in their house in St Margarita. We ate comfortably in the kitchen and I recall that Signora Belgrano had produced from the wood burning stove, a huge dish of what looked like jointed pieces of roast chicken. It was delicious but I did notice that some pieces had an odd shape. They had been wrapped in ham, wonderful prosciutto ham, and slow roasted with herbs, but eventually the penny dropped and I grasped that the dish was half chicken and half rabbit pieces. For me eating rabbit had ceased years ago with the myxomatosis scare, but I learned that the disease had not travelled to Italy and rabbit was a real delicacy there. I can honestly say it was one of the most memorable dishes I have ever eaten, the meat melted off the bones and taste was simply fantastic, and years later I tried to replicate this dish here in England but I have never yet achieved that authentic taste that I had all those years ago in Signora Belgrano's kitchen. Perhaps it was the wood fired oven that made the difference.

6

Marriage

Pepperonata

1 large onion finely chopped
4 red, orange or yellow
peppers, de-seeded and cut
into strips
1 lb tomatoes, chopped
roughly or a tin of chopped
tomatoes.
4 tablespoons of good virgin
olive oil
1tsp dried oregano
Salt & pepper

Serves 2–3

Using half the olive oil, fry
the chopped onion gently
until transparent rather than
brown. Add more oil with the
sliced peppers and turn them
together in the pan making
sure everything is covered in
oil. Fry very gently until the
peppers are quite soft, then
add tomatoes and mix well.
Add the oregano, salt and
pepper and again mix well.
Turn down the heat and let
this mixture simmer for about
twenty minutes making sure
that it is topped up with a little
water if it seems to be drying
out too much.

Allow the pepperonata to cool
a little before serving with
chunks of good bread.

After a wonderful year in Italy, I had reluctantly returned to England at my parents' request. My mother was making herself ill worrying about me. But I returned with the resolve to make friendships with any Italians living in Leeds, so that I could further develop or at least keep up my fluency with the Italian language. I already spoke Italian quite well as Signora Durand and family where I stayed were non-English speakers so it was a matter of my speaking Italian in order to survive! She had been an Italian language teacher before having her family so the Italian she spoke was pure and grammatically correct. Even today when my Italian has grown rusty, people always comment that I speak with a very good accent and with good grammar, all thanks to her.

Back in Leeds one of the Italians I had met was Gino, an immensely talented hairdresser who had opened a small salon in the centre of the city near the famous Jacomelli's, a really good restaurant which unfortunately was later turned into a Berni Inn. It was the day of complicated bouffant hairstyles and Gino was an expert in getting my hair to look really special. I had found a job immediately after returning to England and I was working at Leeds Permanent Building Society in the Advance department. This department had always traditionally employed men, but I was the first "experiment" to see whether women could do the same job. I hope I proved the case for women. But having this job meant I had some money in my pocket again having lived on very little pocket money (£2 per week) during my year in Italy. I could afford to go to the hairdresser once more instead of snipping it myself, so on my weekly visits there we would chat away in Italian and he would sometimes invite me for a coffee in the evenings. Coffee bars were very much in vogue at the time and our favourite venue was the Del Rio on Basinghall Street which was later pulled down to make way for a British Home Store. It was all see through glass cups and saucers and frothy coffee. One evening he said "I am too small to be your boyfriend (I am five foot ten inches and he was a good four inches shorter) so I will introduce you to my friend as he is much taller." Enter Vittorio, a classically good-looking Italian, who was working in the kitchen at the Queens Hotel, Leeds. And he was at least six foot tall. This new friendship with Vittorio progressed over the next year or so and we eventually got engaged around the time of my twenty-first birthday.

To digress for a moment, celebrating the twenty-first birthday in those days was a grand occasion. Nobody celebrated an eighteenth birthday. My parents wanted to give me a celebration to remember so they had decided to invite all the family and my friends to a sit-down evening meal at the Astoria, which had a restaurant with a suite of rooms attached to one of the major ballrooms in the city. We had been over to the venue in Roundhay Road to inspect menus etc. and Mum had chosen a chicken main course. The day arrived. I was done up in a new dress for the occasion, a sophisticated pale blue affair with a separate panel at the front and back as a sort of over-skirt. There was a sherry reception, then I and my parents, Vittorio, and about thirty friends and family filed through to the restaurant for our meal. The starter went without problem – the ubiquitous prawn cocktail which was a classic dish of the sixties, and we awaited our chicken main course. The waiters arrived with platters of chicken breasts and legs covered in a sauce with a boiled rice border. My mother took one look and immediately claimed that we were being served the wrong meal. The Head Waiter was summoned and he assured her that this was what she had ordered – Chicken a la King. Of course to my parents this description would have meant nothing as they were not familiar with restaurant food and the names of different dishes – they would have thought that the "a la King" tag meant it was especially good roast chicken. However Vittorio, from his Queens Hotel service experience, knew the dish and confirmed that this was indeed what Chicken a la King was, and my mother had to back down. In fact I remember it as a very tasty meal and I enjoyed it. After all I was quite used to eating rice as a savoury dish in Italy, but Mum was mortified at offering our guests pieces of chicken in a sauce with boiled rice instead of a nice roast chicken! To her the only use for rice was a good rice pudding.

Vittorio and I married in October 1964, but we decided that we should visit his family in Italy to meet them before marrying, rather than going there after the event, *fait accompli*. We planned to spend a whole month, first driving down to Italy then a couple of weeks with them so that I could get to know them properly. The family had a smallholding in Greci, a small village south east of Naples, in the province of Avellino. They had a couple of cows, lots of chickens, grew all their own food and made wine from their own small vineyard – I suppose it was the Italian version of "The Good Life", except that this was the way most rurally-housed Italians existed in southern Italy.

We arrived hot and tired after a long two or three day drive from England, and after a welcoming meal I realised that even with my improved Italian, I could not understand what they were saying as they spoke in a local dialect based on Albanian. I fell into bed for a well-deserved sleep. I didn't wake until nine the next day and as I lay in bed coming round, I realised there was a wonderful smell of cooking. I was hoping it might be my breakfast so I had a quick wash in the outside cold water trough which ran from the nearby spring, (no hot water here then!) and went to the table. I could not believe my eyes. At just after nine in the morning, Vittorio's father and sisters were sitting having a huge meal and there were at least five bottles of their own red wine on the table ready for drinking. Wine for breakfast? What I realised later was that my prospective father-in-law and Vittorio's two sisters, Luisa and Antonietta, had started work in the fields well before six that morning before it was too hot to work in the August heat, and so they had returned for what seemed to them like a well deserved lunch, and naturally with lunch you drank wine. Their wine was a heavy, dry red variety and it certainly packed a punch, but for me — still relatively unused to wine of any type as the Durands were a non-drinking family — it was knockout material and after that first breakfast with the family I felt like going back to my bed.

There were also thick hand-cut slices of home-cured ham, warmed in the pan, and this was my first taste of good olive oil being used to fry my two freshly laid eggs. At the first taste I was unsure whether I could eat eggs fried in olive oil but I soon got used to it and now I would never fry eggs in anything else, and the smell of eggs frying in fragrant virgin olive oil always takes me back to that first breakfast. The bread was a very heavy country variety which was made by Vittorio's sister Luisa each week and the huge round loaves, perhaps eighteen inches across, were baked in the village communal oven. I loved it on the first or second day after baking, with its crunchy outer crust and its doughy inside, but at three or four days old when it was a little less fresh, your teeth had to be very strong to chew through it. At that stage it was often used to soak up the broth of *minestra*, a less heavy version of minestrone, or as a base of salad when it was chopped into pieces, drizzled with olive oil and places in the bottom of the dish before all the leaves etc were put on top, then tossed together for a delicious taste.

As I ate my breakfast I had chance to look around properly, for the night before I had been too tired to take it in and it had been too dark. No electricity there either, just rock gas produced from a piece of lava rock that was immersed in water in a can, and then the gas given off was lit. I saw that hanging from the rafters of the farmhouse were dozens of hams as well as lots of provolone cheeses, locally called *caciocavalli or scammozze*. These cheeses in their hard state were cut into slices and eaten after the meal, but in the fresh state were what we would now recognise as white buffalo mozzarella. These fresh versions were so wonderful eaten at lunch as one of the courses. My mother-in-law in those early visits used to make them herself from their own cows milk, and I remember her pulling and stretching the cheese in the whey for ages before she was satisfied with the consistency. Later when she had become too old to do these tasks she always made sure that she sent for the freshest mozzarella she could find from surrounding farms ready for my visit, as she knew this was my absolute favourite.

The hams were not all their own production but my in-laws acted as a sort of sales outlet for many of the outlying smallholdings, because their farm was right next to the main road which meant that "townies" travelling towards Foggia, the nearest large town, would call by and ask to buy a cheese or a ham or fresh eggs. My in-laws always gave assurances that they were selling the very freshest of eggs, but I had a suspicion that the freshest eggs always landed on our table!

In one of the familiar TV adverts featuring Italian products you will see the idyllic picture of a large Italian family sitting outside for a meal under the shade of the vines. Well that is exactly how it was in Greci, with one startling difference. Their outside patch was across the road from the farm gates, so everything including table, chairs and dishes had to be carried across the road to be laid out before the meal, dashing between traffic with every item needed. The preparation took a good hour. Then course by course, all the food was transported across, dish by dish, and the usual bottles of wine, but when we all finally sat down – perhaps a dozen of us together – then all the effort was worthwhile.

Visiting Greci in August meant I got to taste the most wonderful pepper dishes, particularly the *pepperonata* which was a gloriously colourful melange of red, orange and yellow peppers cooked slowly in their usual heavy olive oil and eaten with chunks of their good country bread. This is another dish that I have cooked probably hundreds of times over the years, and hot or cold, it's always fabulous.

My favourite meat is lamb, but I was not prepared for how I got it on my first Greci visit. As you can imagine, their youngest son bringing home his future wife was definitely a "kill the fatted calf" occasion, but actually it wasn't a calf but a lamb. We all set off for the weekly market in the village, and to my horror we bought a lamb that trotted home behind us. I knew that if I touched it or even looked at it in its cute state, I would not want to eat it later, so I resolutely refused all contact that day. Next morning when I got up the deed was done. Antonietta, Vittorio's older sister, apparently always did the butchering, and it was all jointed ready for the oven. I learned over the years to accept that this is the way of life on a farm, but the first time did make me feel rather squeamish.

There were so many dishes that I tasted for the first time on that month in Greci, many using ingredients I had never seen before but all were fantastic fresh tastes that can't be replicated with ingredients bought from the supermarket. The pasta was often hand rolled on a big board on Mother-in-law's knee. They had a speciality in that area called "*orecchiete*" – little ears – and they looked just like their name. I tried to learn how to do it but to get perfect shapes takes years of practice. There were green vegetables I had not seen before called "*cavallo nero*", another ingredient that is now available over here. They were either cooked in broth or fried in pieces in olive oil. And of course the fruit came fresh from the trees – nectarines, peaches and apricots, as well as a strange fruit they called "*nespoli*" that looked like an apricot but was very sweet and juicy but with treacherous juice that stained linen black so there when eating this fruit, there was a need to be very careful. What a wonderful month of new food experiences that was.

7

Cooking up a Storm

Family Circle & OXO

Cook of the Year Competition

REGIONAL WINNER

This certificate is presented to

Mrs Popra

who in the opinion of the judges, is a Regional Winner in 'Cook of the Year' Competition

Date

Signed Christine Brody Editor

Family Circle

In the early years after we married, I had given birth to my two daughters. Marina had been born in 1966 just eighteen months after we were married and unfortunately my pregnancy had put paid to the first joint catering venture that we had embarked on. We'd bought a sandwich bar in Harrogate with the idea of running it between us. We prepared dozens of sandwiches for the daily lunchtime rush and I baked apple pies and cakes in the afternoon for the teatime tourists. My love for simple sliced cheddar cheese and tomato sandwiches dates from this period. We had limited preparation space so it limped along but it was providing us with a living. When I discovered I was having our first baby I was overjoyed but one month later realised my body was not as pleased as I was, and had so much pain in my back that it was eventually recommended that I spent the rest of my pregnancy encased in a straightjacket. I couldn't move except to lie flat so that meant no work, and wages to pay someone else to do my stint. The business was not strong enough to stand that outgoing cost so just after Marina was born we sold it on and Vittorio found a job again in Leeds. Our second daughter Anna was born three years later and life carried on as before, with me topping up the household total income by working part-time.

During the short ownership of the Harrogate sandwich bar, there was one memory that will always stick out in my mind. We had taken over the place in February and a couple of months later we were contacted by a company who were going to have a trade stand at the Great Yorkshire Show, also in Harrogate. It was their usual practice to supply sandwiches on a hospitality basis for all the visitors to their stand. Having heard of us (the new kids on the block) he wanted a quote to supply three hundred rounds of ham sandwiches for each of the three days of the show. Vittorio totted up the possibilities, we made a quote and it was accepted. When the week of the show arrived, we set up an evening conveyor belt in the kitchen, roping in my mother and her friend to help with the buttering of endless loaves of bread. What we had not considered was how we were to transport three hundred sandwiches each day that would not fit easily into our small saloon car we were running at the time. We put as many loaded bread trays as was possible into the boot and the back seat, but a couple were destined to be covered and strapped to a roof rack as the only means of getting them there.

At six thirty the first morning we set off from Leeds in order to get into the showground before the deadline of eight o'clock. As we expected there were queues of traffic already at that early hour and we had just reached the front of the queue ready to turn right through the gates when the policeman on duty put up his hand to stop us. Vittorio applied the brakes and as a result the two trays of sandwiches on top of the car shot forward and spilled onto the bonnet, the road and all around. We jumped out of the car trying to pick up what we could and move on quickly as we were causing such a hold up, while everyone who drove around us made scathing remarks and laughed. It could have been a scene straight out of a Carry On film. Was my face red! To crown it all, the guy in charge of the stand was one of those who passed us as we were clearing the mess and his first words to us as we arrived were, "And I don't want any of those that have been on the floor!" But he saw the funny side of it too when it was all over, and he paid up without any quibble as we gave such good value for money.

And so to 1972, and after being married for over seven years, I had discovered that one of the most annoying things about being married to a chef, was that no matter how well I myself cooked, everyone always assumed that he had done it and not me. It was infuriating! I had been growing more keenly interested in food and how to prepare it. I had always collected cuttings from magazines since being a teenager, although recipes in magazines in those days were not full of modern ingredients such as lemon grass, walnut oil or balsamic vinegar. They were plain wholesome ingredients such as mince beef and cabbage, and to vary from the way we had all had been taught to cook the dish at school, meant merely that the accompanying picture of a Shepherds Pie was varied by a few daintily sliced tomatoes and a forked topping to the mashed potatoes! But my repertoire was growing. I avidly read the new colour cookbooks produced by Paul Hamlyn, and had discovered Elizabeth David who to my mind changed the way we thought about food in Britain. Her book about Mediterranean food brought back memories of all the delights I had sampled in Italy and it is still one of my treasured volumes on the cookbook shelf.

In the recipe sections in magazines – in particular Family Circle, a magazine sold alongside its sister magazine

Living, in grocery supermarkets, there were now beginning to be lots of inspiring ideas that were easy to follow for would-be cooks. Family Circle had an annual competition to find their own Cook of the Year and in 1972 I sent in my entry supplying the required "helpful hint which was both economical and creative" according to the rules. The competition was co-sponsored by Oxo and the Gas Board, so later rounds would need to include Oxo as an ingredient, but for this eliminator, it was not necessarily required. My "tip" was to suggest mincing down the remains of the Sunday joint, adding a spoonful of Oxo gravy to make it easier to spread, and use the result as sandwich fillings for work. I will now confess for the first time, that I invented the idea without ever trying the result to see how it tasted. Nevertheless, weeks later I received a phone call to tell me that I had earned a place in the North East England finals of the competition, and I had to cook my way towards the London final by competing against eleven other finalists in a cook-off evening at Leeds Town Hall. Reaching this stage also meant I had won £20 plus a couple of prizes, and £20 was quite a lot of money in 1972.

Cooking in the next round meant I had to come up with a totally new recipe idea of which one of the ingredients had to be – yes you've guessed it – an Oxo cube, although by now there was a chicken variety and not just the red and silver foil-wrapped beef flavour. I remember lying awake at night combing through all my ideas, planning my strategy, a habit which I have retained to this day. Vittorio made lots of suggestions but to my mind they were all based too strongly on his training in well-known classic dishes, and were not new and innovative. I was looking for something special that had not been done before. I eventually came up with something called

"Flamenco Pork Chops", a dish with a solid British ingredient as its base, but given a continental twist. The chops were to be coated first in beaten egg, then tossed in a mixture of homemade breadcrumbs and a crumbled Chicken Oxo cube, then lightly fried until golden brown. That was the "traditional with a twist" element.

The unusual bit was what I had planned to accompany the pork chops, in that I specified cooking a ratatouille with red peppers, courgettes, onions and tomatoes, which would provide the bed for the chops and the border of the dish would be chopped raw celery to give a contrasting crunch against the softer smooth taste of the ratatouille. This suggestion made Vittorio scoff saying, "But you must have a border of duchesse potatoes not raw celery. Nobody uses raw celery". I tried to tell him that was exactly the point but being a classically trained chef, he couldn't agree at all. Finally I would then serve a tomato sauce given a shot with another Chicken Oxo cube, instead of the usual British gravy. I remember arguing all of these ingredients with Vittorio who could only think in terms of what a grand dish would be bordered with at the Queens Hotel, where he worked, but I stuck to my guns.

I tried out the dish on several of our friends and recall almost losing a couple of them who after eating my meal proclaimed it excellent, but then adding "Of course it ought to be good with Vittorio advising you. You don't need to think of anything yourself". I was livid and even more determined to win. I started to think about what I could do to give me an edge over the other competitors and decided to use various "props" to present my dish on the night − a long length of bright red cloth, a pair of castanets and a much used Spanish language book would be placed on the table around my dish to add to the "Flamenco" flavour of its name. I admit that by this point I had become highly competitive!

I arrived at Leeds Town Hall with all my ingredients, lists as long as a French baguette, and loads of confidence – my signature tune! At the given signal all twelve of us began, each one working in her own small kitchen, which had been rigged up on stage in front of a packed audience. I had my lists pinned before me, and prepared and chopped to a rigid plan. I remember one judge, Grace Allen, a rather well known regional cook, commenting on my organisation, "Goodness me your bench looks so streamlined and orderly but it obviously works well for you". She was most impressed.

Everything went together like a dream that night, virtually nothing went wrong and at the end of the cooking time I set my colourful dish of food onto its Spanish setting and stood back thinking I might be in with a chance. The results were announced at the end of the evening and I waited with my heart thumping away. "And the winner this evening who will go on to cook in the London final is Margaret Poppa". I'd won and all my sleepless nights and arguments had not been in vein. I was now going to represent the North East at the next stage.

The format for cooking in the London final was the preparation of a main course, which could be the same dish presented in the regional heats, and a pudding to finish. We would have two hours to prepare and cook the meal. Again twelve contestants competing together, but we were also to be televised for Southern Regional TV and the whole affair to be compered by Michael Aspel. Quite a big affair then! I decided to stick with the

Flamenco Pork chops, but I wanted something unusual to finish. I eventually decided on a rice dish – what I suppose was cold rice pudding with additions but it had the grand name of Tutti-frutti Rice and I made the recipe with lots of cream and added green, yellow and red glace cherries and flaked almonds. The finishing touch to this un-moulded rice delight was supposed to be piped double cream, but the heat of the TV lights was my downfall and I could not get the cream to stay whipped on the night. Unfortunately it was not my night, and I did not win in the final. I saw the prize go to a woman who could obviously cook anything, probably even make a couple of eggs and a small bag of flour into a fabulous three tier wedding cake in one hour flat, and she was a well-deserved winner. She had cooked a chicken pie with a difference as the content (a whole boned chicken stuffed with herbs), was encased in a golden shortcrust pastry chicken that looked, (and apparently tasted) absolutely wonderful. The second prize-winner was the only man competing in the final and his dish was a colourful savoury rice dish with a dry martini sauce. Looking at all the finished dishes, I judged I came somewhere around fourth place in the twelve but I did have £200 and various prizes from the sponsors such as food hampers, pans, cookbooks etc. And of course, a memorable experience as well as the knowledge that at least I had proved that I could do it myself without the help of a chef/husband.

As a result of winning the regional final, I was asked to do a short five-minute recipe spot on Radio Leeds each week, which I was thrilled about. Cooking on radio simply meant that every stage of a recipe had to be described as to how it should look at that point, as there were no viewing windows for the listeners. I'm lucky that, unlike many people, performing in any way does not give me nerves at all. Not long after, while I was still doing the radio programme, Yorkshire TV put out a call for guests to cook on their new series "Farmhouse Kitchen". Using my spot on Radio Leeds to introduce myself, I was asked to prepare an audition which would be me cooking at home in my own kitchen, talking through what I was doing to the couple of observing programme producers. Excitedly looking forward to my big break, I started to get my ideas together and then suddenly found (to my great surprise I might add) that I was pregnant with our third child.

Unfortunately pregnancy for me, on all three occasions, was "can't look at food for at least three months without being ill", so the timing was totally wrong and the opportunity had to be passed up. So instead of cooking up a storm on TV I sat on the settee, sipping water and eating plain crackers, while I watched the series develop into one of the successes of the decade, and a forerunner to the dozens of cooking programmes that followed. Oh well!

8
Miller
Howe

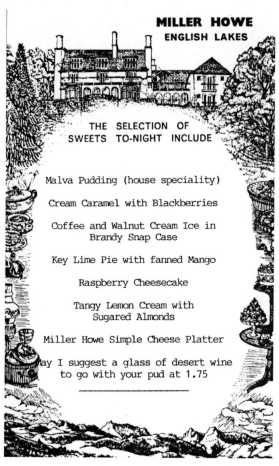

MILLER HOWE
ENGLISH LAKES

THE SELECTION OF
SWEETS TO-NIGHT INCLUDE

Malva Pudding (house speciality)

Cream Caramel with Blackberries

Coffee and Walnut Cream Ice in
Brandy Snap Case

Key Lime Pie with fanned Mango

Raspberry Cheesecake

Tangy Lemon Cream with
Sugared Almonds

Miller Howe Simple Cheese Platter

May I suggest a glass of desert wine
to go with your pud at 1.75

Sadly for all of us, my husband and I split up in 1975, having gradually grown apart. Looking back I believe that no matter how good my Italian was and how polished Vittorio's English was, we never knew each other well enough before we married. It's very difficult to really get to know someone who speaks another language. The most difficult thing to grasp is the sense of humour in a foreign language, and really there were differences between us that I couldn't have initially detected but were more about cultural differences and what we wanted from life. I was always ambitious and impatient to put my new ideas into practice, whereas Vittorio is hard working, very family-orientated and was usually happy with the status quo. These differences increasingly plunged me into a state of unhappiness, and there was often tension and arguments generally. I'm sure there were good times too but eventually I took the view that long-term it would be better for our children not to grow up in the midst of arguments even if there was to be hardship, and we separated. The next few years were a hard slog. Richard had been born in 1973 so it meant bringing up three young children alone, but that had been my choice. Happily, after the first few months, there was less animosity between us, and the children were able to keep a strong relationship going with their father, but it wasn't always a happy time for me. I often questioned whether I had worked hard enough at keeping the marriage going and whether I should have taken the decision I did. Gradually over those years, I moved from working a few part-time hours within school times, as many young mums do, to the beginnings of a new career in recruitment as the children grew up, which meant there was a bit more money to spend. But largely the next ten years were a round of work, childrearing, and little social life other than church activities such as drama groups and ladies' meetings.

However, in 1985 I met someone new, Michael, and in the following year when I moved house, he eventually moved in with us. The family then was two teenagers plus me, as Marina had gone off to University in London, soon to be followed by Anna on the same trail. That year when my birthday came round in May, Michael planned a surprise for me. My love of cooking had never gone away, it had simply been buried for a while under the needs of three children who wanted to eat sausages and chips or spaghetti bolognese. Nor had my penchant for buying cookery books disappeared. A favourite of the time was John Tovey, a chef who owned and ran a hotel in the Lake District. He used to appear regularly as a guest on TV programmes, and he was known for his rather showy (and rather rich!) style of cooking. He was typical of the style of eating in the eighties which today we would regard as most unhealthy in its overuse of rich dairy products.

Just as today I might want to dine at the Bray restaurant of the celebrated Heston Blumenthal, it was one of my cherished wishes in those years, to eat at John Tovey's hotel in Windermere. Going out for a meal had started to become something most people did on a fairly regular basis, but we didn't have anywhere locally that I knew of, that could compare to John Tovey's cooking. So back to the birthday surprise. I was told that we were to have a couple of days away that weekend while the children stayed with their father, and I soon found myself in the car heading for the Lake District. After a couple of hours driving in glorious sunshine through the Yorkshire Dales, we suddenly pulled into the grounds of an hotel and I realised we were at the famous Miller Howe, the establishment owned by John Tovey. I imagined that at long last my dream of having afternoon tea there on the lawns overlooking Lake Windermere, was to come true, and that we would then move on to somewhere more in our price bracket to stay. But no! Bags came out of the car (perhaps not the quality of luggage that accompanied most of their arriving hotel guests) and I was ushered into the hotel and eventually to our room. I don't think I have ever been silent for so long. I was totally unable to say a word being so taken unawares. I could not believe that not only was I having afternoon tea, I was going to sample dinner and breakfast too, and hopefully every dish would look as if it came right out of the pages of his cookbooks!

The whole weekend was a very memorable three days, starting with the magnificent view from the picture window in our room. My partner had not stinted on the cost – if we were going to do it, we would do it right! Every room was named after one of the lakes and we were given Elterwater, a premium room on the first floor, at the front of the hotel, with it own wide balcony overlooking the wonderful expanse of water that was Windermere. It was idyllic. At that stage of my life, I had never stayed in an hotel anything like as luxurious as this was, and I wallowed in the prettiness of it all –

very reminiscent of the Laura Ashley style, with every whim provided for. I sat and had my afternoon tea on the terrace, eating deliciously light scones with fragrant thick cream and strawberry jam, feeling every inch a lady-who-lunches, and then I wiled away the couple of hours leafing through magazines and gazing at the view, until it was time to dress and go down for dinner, which by all accounts was to be a theatrical performance as well as a gourmet meal.

All the guests were requested to assemble in the sitting room or salon adjoining the dining room at seven sharp ready for the seven thirty start of the evening. Cocktails and canapés were offered and we partook, although I was so overwhelmed I have no idea what I drank, but it would most likely have been a perfectly mixed G & T. Precisely at seven thirty on the dot, the lights in the dining room were lowered and a hush fell over the room as the Head Waiter announced that dinner was served. The diners filed into the room and we found ourselves seated at one of several tables by the window overlooking the lake (it appeared that if you booked the best bedrooms the staff accordingly allocated to you the best window tables) where we could watch the beautiful late evening sky. Each table had a menu of what Master Chef, John Tovey, would cook for us that evening. There was to be no customer choice until we reached the dessert course, it was a set menu of five courses pre-selected for us. When I say it was a theatrical performance those are the right words, as from the first announcement, we became part of it and as the lights were lowered, we made our way to the dining room. Each course was preceded by the choreographed entrance of several smartly attired waiters all simultaneously presenting the dishes to the diners with flourish. Periodically, lights changed according to the effect desired and the meal finished with a grand tour of the dining room by John Tovey himself, chatting to every customer and making sure that everything had given satisfaction.

It was perfection and of course I saved the menu from that evening so I can tell you every detail of what we ate. First an unusual starter of autumn fruits served with cheese flavoured sablés (biscuits), followed by a beef consommé with mushroom garnish and diced apple. Then a very light fish course, which was prawn and smoked salmon slice with caviar, served on cucumber yoghurt and accompanied by lemon buttered brown bread. The main course may have seemed more ordinary as it was roast chicken but it had been cooked with thyme, honey and lemon and was served on a puree made from the chicken liver flavoured with sage, and had with it small portions of seven different vegetables. Finally we moved on to the puddings and for this course we were presented with a second menu and the option to choose and at that stage, being so full, I selected the lightest item, which was rum and raisin ice cream in a brandy snap case. We moved back to the salon for coffee and petit fours but not before we had our own two minutes of conversation with the famous chef himself.

He asked us which part of the meal we had particularly enjoyed and I found myself saying, "Everything was wonderful but I particularly enjoyed the butter we had with our bread rolls. It has such an unusual taste." John Tovey seemed to be quite impressed by my singling out such a small ingredient and his reply was "We try so hard to make every small element of the meal just right, and that butter came from the herd of Jerseys that are owned by a neighbouring farmer just down the road.

I'm so glad you liked it." It was obvious throughout the weekend that every consideration was given to smallest items such as the butter so that there would be a fabulous overall effect.

That weekend was memorable and strangely enough when people asked me later what I had most enjoyed eating, I always nominated the breakfast porridge which preceded the Miller Howe English Breakfast Grill. Porridge there was like no other ever tasted, and the milk they used was also supplied courtesy of the Jersey herd down the road, and in later years when I owned my own tea-rooms, I used this recipe in our Sunday morning brunches. How was it different? Well the oats and creamy milk sat overnight in the warming drawer of the oven, then next morning after being cooked until soft and squidgy, it was served with butter, more cream if desired, and a dash of whisky. We later named it boozy porridge, and people certainly asked for more. On the middle day of the weekend, the Saturday, we toured around the lakes in the car and the hotel even provided a boxed picnic for us. We settled to eat it in a leafy place overlooking yet another lake and found that it contained a miniature meal lovingly prepared with small delights such as cream cheese pate, exotic fruit salad and home-baked ham, all beautifully packed in their own small containers. A truly upper class picnic.

I was to visit Miller Howe again twice – once for another week-end stay, and then also for their wonderful cookery course, which as it lasted for five days, was almost overwhelming by the time you reached the end. Eating at that level for a two-night weekend stay is ample for anyone. I remember leaving feeling stuffed like the chicken we had been served on our first evening, and each time I also left with a signed cookbook of his recipes. When not at work in the kitchen he was usually to be found in his cubby-hole of an office under the stairs with his adoring Old English sheepdog lying at his feet. John Tovey eventually retired to his beloved South Africa and sold Miller Howe to new owners. I have never been back there since, but I hear that some of his theatrical touches have been preserved.

9

Tuscany

Recipe for Tuscan "Fave e Pecorino"

(salad of broad beans and pecorino cheese)

1 kilo of very young small
tender broad beans (or 2 kilo
of larger beans)
4 oz pecorino cheese
olive oil & lemon juice
handful of fresh basil leaves.

In Italy in April there is a short
season when the broad beans
are young and tender enough
to eat all including the pods. If
you grow your own and catch
the season do try it, otherwise
later in the season shell the
beans, wash and place in a
salad bowl. Shave thin pieces
of pecorino on top and scatter
basil leaves. Mix olive oil and
lemon juice to your taste and
pour over. Toss together well
and serve.

From my days as an *au pair* in Genova, Italy was firmly established as my *alma mater* in respect of food and how to cook. I had taken the Mediterranean style of eating to my heart and even nowadays all of my dinner-party entertaining has an Italian flavour about it somewhere. I always feel that it has sun, love and life embodied in its every part. The TV series featuring Jamie Oliver – "An Italian Adventure" – seemed to say that he felt this way too. The Italians themselves have such an inbuilt love of food that is so natural to them, whether they are rich or poor. For them it's all about making the best of whatever ingredients they have, and preparing everything with love and care.

So it's no wonder that in the eighties, when people were talking of Tuscany as a desirable holiday venue, (well before Tony Blair decided to holiday there), I decided I had to have a holiday in that region as for me it remained undiscovered. When I was married, going to Italy as a family used always to start with the long drive down through France, over the mountains via the Mont Blanc tunnel and at last into Aosta to start the descent into northern Italy, and I would gradually be able to get the feel of being back in a country which I would happily adopt as my second home. The Aosta valley always took me back to the holiday weeks in August that I spent with the family Durand during my year's stay in Italy in 1962, when typical of all Italian city dwellers, they escaped to the cooler temperatures of the foothills of the Alps. The whole family – grandmother and grandfather Durand, my family who were Lilia and Piervaldo Durand and their three children, and the younger brother, also Piervaldo, squashed together in their rambling old family house in Torre Pelice, in the area known as the protestant valley of Italy, Val d'Aosta. Because there were so many of us, I was allocated a small bedroom above one of the outbuildings in the garden, and each night I would trip down the path after dinner and after the children were in bed. One night, after a pleasant evening of home-made musical entertainment, when I climbed the stairs and switched on the light there was a huge flying insect in the room which I proceeded to chase around with a rolled up newspaper. Suddenly, the three men of the family came rushing up the stairs. They had seen the light go on through my curtains and had then watched as I manically chased something round with my arms waving. They assumed that there was an intruder and had gallantly come to my aid, but when they saw what was actually happening, we all laughed about it, and I was not allowed to forget it.

Although I no longer do this, on long continental drives I always used to smoke my duty-free cigarettes on the drive down through France and Italy, even though at home I had ceased being a smoker years before – it was one of my holiday rituals, something to do with being in a car with an open sun roof, windows down and lots of carefree sunshine – a Thelma and Louise moment. After the mountains around Turin, the road slowly descends to the Italian Riviera and skirts around Genova where my Italian connection had started. Then starts the winding road along the Riviera coast which used to be known as Il Brago (the caterpillar) until it was replaced by a motorway on stilts which carved its way through hills and valleys alike, and in doing so, cut out all the hairpin bends, twists and turns. Reaching Pisa means you have broken the back of the journey, and then from Pisa it is just a hop, skip and a jump to anywhere in Tuscany.

However for some reason, on my first trip to Tuscany with my partner at the time, Michael, it was decided that there was not time for the leisurely drive through France and Northern Italy, and if we wanted to spend a full two weeks relaxing in the Tuscan sun, it would be much better if we took a flight to Pisa, then got ourselves a hire-car for the last stage of the journey to the village of San Donato in Poggio, where we had rented an apartment for two weeks. As I spoke fluent Italian I imagined that after landing at Pisa airport late afternoon, we would have ample time for a leisurely drive to the village in our hire-car, stopping to pick up some delicious food supplies on the way in small markets or at the roadside. Unfortunately I had not taken flight delays into my calculations and we landed at Pisa airport hours after we should have done, finally had our luggage stowed in our hire-car and the paper work completed, then drove as fast as was feasible to find our holiday apartment. For those of you who have not driven in the countryside in Tuscany at night, (and there may be a few) driving down the main highways is fine but as soon as you leave those behind, you are in complete inky black darkness and need to crawl along if you are looking for anywhere for the first time, as the signs are somewhat overgrown and hidden and on a non-starry night there are no lights at all to guide you on your way. This was such a night and we eventually reached the village well after eleven, threw the luggage into the apartment, and not having eaten all day and with not one morsel of food between us, we set off to find food – anything to stave off the hunger pangs!

There were a few street lights in the village so we eventually found the "sell everything" village shop but it was all closed up for the night, and even the local bar was shuttered and quiet, and it looked as if we had a long night ahead of us without so much as a cup of tea. Then I noticed that there was a small restaurant along the street from us where they were just noisily bidding goodnight to their last customers. I sprinted (I could sprint in those days) along to their door before they had chance to shoot the bolts into place for the night. I just managed to catch the door before it completely closed, asking the Signora who stood there if there was any possibility of eating even one course with them, hurriedly trying to also explain why we were so late, that we had nothing in the house etc. In short, in my rather hesitant untried-for-ten-years Italian, which usually improved over the following two weeks as I got into the swing of the language again, I threw myself on her mercy. It worked and her inbuilt sense of hospitality won the day. She invited us into the restaurant's main area, a high-ceilinged long room, saying that if we wanted to join them and their staff in the meal that they usually ate after everyone had gone home, then we were welcome. The format apparently was that they would always share out whatever was left that night after the service. We were lucky because that night they had served rabbit cooked in a fabulous rich peasant stew, a dish that is a typical way to use the game that Tuscan hunters are so fond of shooting. We both loved rabbit as it is cooked on the continent – usually with lots of garlic and vegetables and red wine, and cooked until it is very tender and succulent. Gently steaming plates were put before us. We ate as if we had never seen food before, finishing off the magnificent helping of stew by mopping up every drop of *sugo* (rich dark sauce) with pieces of their home-made country bread. When she heard the full story of why we were delayed, and the fact that we had no provisions at all, the restaurant owner insisted that we take some bread and milk for morning so that we could have a decent breakfast before bustling off to get the shopping in. What hospitable people the Italians are.

Needless to say we went back several times over the next two weeks to eat from the wonderful menu that they had there. I don't think anything ever quite came up to that wonderful rabbit dish that we had the first evening and it is a memory that always comes back to me whenever I see rabbit on any restaurant menu.

That trip to Tuscany confirmed every travel article I had ever read of it being a beautiful region of Italy. Perhaps the reason that the English have taken so strongly to the area is the fact that in many parts its green rolling hills remind them of home, but with excellent food thrown in. This is the region where Pecorino, the beautifully flavoured sheep cheese comes from, in all its variations. There are markets where one stall will display perhaps a couple of dozen different types of Pecorino, from the very freshest soft version made only the day before, to the aged, hard-rinded version that has been sitting maturing for several years. One of my favourite Tuscan dishes is *Fave e Pecorino* a dish of the earliest tender broad beans eaten in their soft green pods with thin slices of Pecorino cheese on top, and served as a starter to a meal. The season for this dish is very short, perhaps just three weeks at the end of April and early May, when after that the bean pods toughen too much to be eaten alongside their contents, so it's very unusual to come across this dish on any menu. I finally managed to sample it on another visit to Tuscany, when we visited a restaurant where a wedding party were celebrating in a private room. I was watching the platters of food being taken in to their festivities and I spotted the plates of tiny broad bean pods with cheese. I asked our waiter if this was indeed the famous *Fave e Pecorino* and he was so impressed that I, a mere tourist, had heard of the dish, that he brought us a platter to try. It was very unusual and so good, with fresh young beans complemented by the salty taste of fresh cheese. Tuscan people are known to be the "bean-eaters" of Italy with their famous white bean soup, another strong regional dish.

Although the regional city that gets all the attention is Florence, for me the city of Siena with its flaming pinkish red brick architecture is every bit as beautiful. The huge round open forum, the Piazza del Campo, where the famous annual race horse race, "Il Palio" takes place, has a surface of these red bricks placed in an immaculate herring-bone formation. Sitting there as a tourist sipping a mid-morning cappuccino (Italians never drink cappuccino after breakfast), you can imagine the clatter of horses' hooves as they course round and round the square with every rider garbed in the bright colours of their own local association and each trying to win the honour for his club. Siena's contribution to the culinary menu is a sweet chewy confection packed with dried fruits and nuts called *panforte* (strong bread). It's a bit too sweet for me but it's the ideal gift to bring for friends back home.

For many tourists the region's Chianti wine is a big attraction but for me this wine is lower down on my list of favourites. In fact although local wines in Tuscany are often rich and ripe with fruit, I find that some of the famous wine varieties such as Chianti and Brunello di Montalcino are not really to my taste. Not everything is perfect, even in Italy.

10

Fundraising
Dinners

Stuffed Vine Leaves (Dolmades)

1 tin/pack of vine leaves in brine
1 medium onion
1 cup of long grain rice
2 cups water
handful of fresh mint leaves, flat
leaf parsley, dill.
1 oz pine nuts
2 oz currants
olive oil

Finely chop the onion in olive oil
until transparent but not brown.
Add rice and stir to cover with oil.
Add water and put lid on the pan
and cook very gently until tender
– about 15 minutes – check near
end of time to make sure not too
dry, if it is add a little more water.
Remove cooked vine leaves
from tin/pack and wash under
running tap to remove the brine.
Chop the fresh herbs finely and
add to rice with pine nuts and
currants. Stir well. Place a vine
leaf on the chopping board and
put tablespoon of rice mixture in
the centre and fold vine leaves
into little parcels. Place all the
parcels in a casserole dish, cover
the dish with foil, and put the dish
inside another larger roasting tray
with an inch of water in it. Put the
whole dish/tin in a medium oven
Gas mark 4–5 to heat through
the vine leaves. Serve with Greek
yoghurt

During the mid-eighties, I realised that my youngest child, Richard, was struggling at school. He had had some unusual problems from a very early age, but a modern diagnosis would probably have been that he suffered from Asperger's Syndrome in a mild form. In an attempt to put a bit more fun into his life, and find something that he could feel he was good at, he and I set off one Saturday morning to the Civic Theatre in Leeds, a place that had always been known for its amateur dramatic activities, including theatre groups for young people. Richard had always enjoyed being in the pantomimes at our local church and so we felt that this was one avenue worth exploring.

We tripped up the wide stone back-steps of the old Victorian theatre, up two floors to the top and started to walk along the corridor, listening at each door for whatever activity might be going on. We eventually stopped to listen at one door where sounds of singing were drifting through. We went in. We saw about fifty young people, boys and girls, apparently between ages ten and twenty roughly. Richard was about eleven at the time and was clearly quite entranced, and they were making wonderful sounds, so we sat and listened in until there was a break. Then talking to the two chaps in charge, the Musical and Artistic Directors, Michael Williamson and Jonathan Clift, we learned that we had walked into a rehearsal of Sondheim's "Sweeney Todd" and this group was Leeds Youth Opera, a unique group of young people who performed not only occasional productions written for young people, but they also tackled very successfully, full scale operas.

That morning began a long and happy association with Leeds Youth Opera. For Richard it was somewhere other than school where he could meet young people in an activity that he enjoyed rather than finding it a trial. Although he never achieved major roles, he did now and then play small parts over the years, and was thrilled by those. And as I myself, as his supportive parent, was drawn into the group more and more, I not only developed my own knowledge of classical music, opera in particular, but also made a group of friends among the other parents that today are still my closest pals.

As with most amateur theatre groups, acquiring funds was always a struggle, and as we took on more and more ambitious projects such as Verdi's "Macbeth" or "Nabucco", then fundraising became an arduous task as even in the early nineties we were actually looking at finding approximately sixteen thousand pounds for each production. I, as the then Chairman of the group, undertook to write and approach all the major financial and business institutions prospecting for a grant. and as a result, we always scraped through, but I have always believed that fundraising should also be fun if it's to be successful, so I also came up with an idea that became very popular among the set of our parent supporters.

As I had always catered for large numbers of people from my married days when Vittorio and I had run a small private catering company, inviting twenty or so friends to dine was quite manageable in my view. By this point in the mid eighties I had moved to a large semi-detached Victorian house in Beeston and had started off my own recruitment consultancy business working from home. I had had several years working as Job Centre Manager in various local Leeds offices, and had then gone on to senior level recruitment at PER but this section of the civil service was now to be subject to privatisation with the infamous Robert Maxwell as its new owner. I did not relish the prospect of working for this particular man, so I decided the time was ripe to spread my wings and become self-employed. The house I had bought was big enough to support a fledgling business. I had passed by and known this house from my childhood and when the opportunity to buy it presented itself one day, I jumped in with both feet. Afterwards the only thing I regretted was that I never seemed to have enough money to put the house back in the order that it deserved.

But as my business grew, I decided to build an office suite, attached to one side of the house, and this eventually became a dual-purpose space. Not only did the new main office house three desks, various filing cabinets, telephone and computer systems for me and my two staff, but when this office furniture was stacked and squeezed into the little interview room next door, I then gained a huge space which was ideal for entertaining.

For one opera production, Verdi's "Macbeth", the set crew had built a huge table for the stage set, which became known ever after as "the Macbeth table" and was hired out around various houses for barbecues and parties. My newly built office extension could comfortably seat twenty-two for dinner using the Macbeth table and a miscellany of mismatched, borrowed chairs and benches. And there the fundraising dinner plan began. Every few months or so I would offer twenty two places at my dinner table at £10 per head (remember this was more than fifteen years ago so that was a fair amount) and in return I would provide a themed meal. If I chose a French theme for the evening, then part of the deal was that all the guests had to turn up in some variation of French costume, and so on.

I loved planning these dinner events and in our time we toured Europe gastronomically with meals from France, Italy, Spain, and Greece, before departing for America and later even the West Indies. There was also a memorable Victorian Christmas banquet. As I had more first-hand experience cooking Italian food that was the one that kicked us off and I was determined that on that particular night our friends should learn that Italian food was far more than pasta and pizza. We started with *antipasti*, passing round huge platters of thinly sliced Milano and Napoli salamis, with one of my favourites, delicate slices of pink mortadella speckled with capers and peppercorns. Unfortunately the huge range of ciabattas that we can buy in shops and supermarkets today, didn't exist then, so we had to make do with French bread.

After the *antipasti* came soup and I here stuck to the well-known and served *minestrone*, as it's a robust flavour that stands up to being made in advance. In fact in my view *minestrone* is always better at the second heating (and eating) as the *pastina* (little pasta shapes made especially for soup) in it have swelled to a beautiful size and the herbs have been allowed to ooze out their full flavour overnight. Obviously attempting to cook more than twenty portions of minestrone meant hunting out the huge pans that had been stowed in the garage for several years, but the biggest problem was making room for them on a regular family-sized gas cooker. From *minestrone* we passed on to our main course, which I seem to recall was chicken *cacciatore* (hunter's chicken) another dish requiring a huge pan atop the cooker! Italians always eat salad or vegetables after the meat course so we followed that tradition with a huge tossed green salad before slowing down to finalise our meal with cheese – my Italian favourites are *pecorino* and *gorgonzola* – and then pudding. I had leaned on the services of my ex-husband for this course (thankfully we have been able to remain friends after our divorce) and as he was employed for many years as a sweet chef in one of Leeds' well-known Italian restaurants, the Flying Pizza, I requested a very large bowl of *tiramisu* (translated this means pick-me-up). So ended fundraiser number one, our Italian evening. My dessert contribution was peaches poached in white wine served with thick cream.

I really would struggle to remember all the menus from the various themed dinners which we arranged but one of the really good memories involved the costumes for the French evening, when one of my friends arrived covered in a curly wool fabric suit complete with tail and black nose, looking every inch the chic French poodle being led up the garden path on collar and lead by her husband garbed as a moustachioed French waiter. Later we all trooped outside to have our photographs taken in our various costumes and on one particular photograph we have the famous French poodle and owner alongside our family pet dog, Sam, who was sniffing the impostor in a very suggestive way!

A very successful evening was the Victorian Christmas banquet that we put on and goodness me what a lot of work that involved, as we had so many courses of fish and meat, and cooking at a hot stove in an ankle-length silk dress nipped in at the waist is nothing short of purgatory. For that evening we even had the services of a white-gloved butler, a young actor friend who received the guests at the door, took their cloaks, and then announced the guests individually as they entered the room. My choice for the main course would have been goose, but the exorbitant cost of those birds with the fact that each goose would barely feed four people, presented a logistical problem of getting five or six geese roasted in time for the meal. Instead I opted for mutton, a firm favourite with the Victorians, served usually with a caper sauce. A local butcher was able to source two whole legs of mutton for me and they were then fitted into yet another large pan to be boiled as the recipe prescribed. What I remember more than anything about that evening is the juggling of huge heavy pans across the top of the cooker, and feeling so hot that I could do a really good Victorian swoon at any minute.

For the Greek evening my residing memory will be my decision when planning the meal, that stuffed vine leaves would be home prepared rather than being bought in tins, and realising what a job I had taken on rolling and stuffing approximately one hundred large vine leaves (even though they can be bought separately in tins) with a fine mixture of herbed rice – a very tedious job. Of course Greek salad with its chunky pieces of feta cheese was much easier to prepare, and the sweet course of authentic sticky sweet *baklava* was also laborious with its layer after layer of buttered filo pastry, but the finished result, so well worth the trouble.

Those events were wonderful evenings that are often talked about and remembered in our group of friends, and to aid my memory I have a small library of specialist books entitled "The Cooking of Spain, of Mexico, of Greece etc", – whatever country I had selected to offer my guests. Only recently we were recalling the Spanish evening and not only the food but the fact that one guest turned up in full Spanish traditional dress, sat next to a similarly attired lady and after the first two courses handed out photocopied sheets of the words to the song "Blue Spanish Eyes", apparently the only well-known Spanish song that she could find. Everyone was encouraged to join in with the singing which as the evening progressed became more and more raucous, largely due to the copious amounts of Spanish wine that everyone had consumed. I cannot hear that song now without remembering the number of times we were all dragooned into singing the chorus. Oh, Happy days!

11

The Georgian Tea-rooms

Frangipane Tart

4 oz butter
4 oz caster sugar
4 oz ground almonds
2 large eggs
1 dessert-spoon of plain flour
2–3 drops of almond essence
small tin of pear halves (or
fresh sliced nectarines or
plums)
Apricot jam
Baked pastry case made with
6 oz flour

Mix together eggs and butter
until smooth and creamy. Add
sugar and ground almonds,
then the almond essence.

Pour the mixture into the
pastry case and place sliced
pears or fresh fruit on top.
Bake in moderately hot oven
(gas mark 6) until all the filling
mixture has set firm. Glaze
the surface with a small
amount of apricot jam. Very
good served warm.

The early nineties, and I had just survived the break-up of my second long-term relationship. Michael and I had met in 1985, through a friend of a friend, and we had lived together from a year afterwards, when he moved from Market Weighton to join us at the new house in Beeston Road. By that time, mid eighties, there were three of us living full-time in the house as Marina had stayed on working in London after finishing university, and Anna was off to start her university course, also in London. However the relationship had been difficult in the latter years. There were faults on all sides but as Richard was a teenager and still battling with some problems at school, I looked to Michael to work out some solution between the two of them and come to some mutual understanding. But sadly after quite a few years of effort on all sides, I still found myself being continually between them, and deep down I knew that for the sake of Richard's future development, and for my peace of mind, something had to give. Faced with the choice I had to make, as a mother it was virtually no choice at all. However much I thought of Michael, and at one point we had talked of marrying, Richard was my son and I simply could not abandon him. So the relationship had to come to an end. I had to re-organise my life, and Richard and I tried to re-build some kind of basis for the future.

At the same time my initial contract with the company that had bought out my recruitment consultancy three years previously, was coming to the re-evaluation point. I had gone along with the takeover and had accepted the Director's position, still running the company on the same lines as before the buy-out, with the exception of the fact that I now had to report to a main board. I could no longer come up with an idea and immediately put in into practice. Now, budgets had to be justified, and management meetings were part of the routine although as I discovered, just a charade. If anyone dared to say anything controversial that provoked discussion, they were quietly taken on one side afterwards and told that this meeting was not the place for general discussion! What management meetings were supposed to be for, I never did work out. The Chief Executive and I had had a few spats and at the three-year end I decided that I wanted to leave the group. I had not been happy with the way the board treated some members of staff, it went against my moral principles, so I felt this was a time for my exit before I became one of the casualties.

Leaving with some pay-off money in my pocket, Richard and I took off for a short holiday in Jersey while I looked around for the next opportunity. I knew it would be working for myself again as once you have tasted that freedom it isn't easy to go back to working for someone else. I'd also realised that the most exciting part of working for oneself was having the ideas and having free range to put them into practice. In short, I loved being successful and bucking the trend, and still do to this day. Many folk who are interested in cooking, have held a dream of perhaps one day opening a restaurant, or playing *mein host* behind the bar of a pub. For me the dream had always been to open a tearoom. I started searching through newspaper ads and estate agents' details for opportunities. A few weeks later I found a possibility in the centre of Leeds in the top floor of an antique showroom in Waterloo House, just behind the famous Corn Exchange. The cafe had been operating for several years and the owners were moving on to other things. I went to have a look round. Richard came with me as part of my idea to buy premises was to provide a job for Richard who had done quite a few training courses in catering, but so far had been unable to find work. I was sure that working alongside me he would be able to cope well.

The café had thirty-six covers with small tables in dark red damask, over-covered with lace cloths, in a bright and cosy room decorated in traditional style with various pretty ornaments and old teapots dressing the scene. There was a fairly well-equipped kitchen, and the café was offering a menu that started with coffee and morning snacks, through to providing light lunches, and later in the day moved on to afternoon teas. It was just the type of menu that I could cope with, so after weighing up the financial side, I made an offer and it was accepted. In hindsight, they accepted my offer too quickly which probably means that I paid too much. We made arrangements to spend a couple of weeks observing trade and the general routine with the owners before taking over ourselves in September 1994.

The first week we were left alone we just about got through, although at times I did stop and wonder what on earth had made me chase the dream at this stage in my life. Being over fifty and changing from a largely sedentary job to one that demanded at least twelve hours a day on my feet in a hot kitchen seemed like madness, and indeed I lost a stone and a half in the first six weeks. But we were both soon into the routine. We shopped at cash and carry twice a week, called elsewhere for bread and fresh vegetables each morning before opening, and then my first job was to produce batches of fresh scones so that as my first customers arrived they were just out of the oven and scenting the air with home baking. Richard would be prepping salads and soup vegetables for lunchtime while I served the morning customers. A part time waitress arrived at twelve and stayed for a couple of hours which got us over the busy lunchtime, then I would cope out front for the rest of the afternoon, slipping a few cakes into the oven whenever there was a gap in the trade.

We specialised in truly home-made cakes and pastries so our glass showcase was filled with such delights as rich chocolate cake, iced carrot cake, apple pies, and loaf cakes such as banana cake, ginger cake, date and walnut, and fruit cake, as well as the obligatory fruit scones which would be served with strawberry jam and fresh cream. The favourite pudding was always pear and frangipane fruit tart, a delicious concoction of pastry, almond flavoured filling, and fruit. We had also decided that we would never serve those nasty plastic sachets of jam and butter but instead our cream tea came with portions of jam and cream in small pots. The only down-side to that decision was that I quite quickly realised that some customers liked our small Royal Doulton china pots so much, they took them home instead of leaving them to be washed up. And we also decided that cream teas would have real whipped cream rather than the squirty cream that we kept for piping on the top of a mug of hot chocolate.

The first mad rush we had was for half-term week in October, about a month after we had taken over. By that time we were into our routine and thought we were managing well, and we were when the trade was light and steady, but suddenly we were packed out every day and every hour of the day, with families of Mum and Dad and all the children, and it was a different ball-game. I well remember one particular day when the part-timer called in sick and we had a full house with every table shouting they were next to be served. In the kitchen we were running out of prepped food, clean crockery and cutlery, and I felt like running into the kitchen and hiding. But we got through it, emergency help arrived in the shape of my Saturday staff who were all at school themselves and glad of extra hours, and the next time we had a rush, on the pre-Christmas shopping build up, we were ready and prepared. Here I must mention our Saturday staff as they were virtually all young members of Leeds Youth Opera, who would attend rehearsals at the theatre until twelve o'clock, then hare through Leeds to join us fifteen minutes later just as the rush was building up, and would then work through the afternoon. Parents and friends at the opera group also supported us with their custom and there was regularly a large table of them all eating Saturday lunch together.

As yet we had changed little from the way it had been running previously. The cake display cabinet was crammed with all the cakes and fruit pies and they seemed as popular as ever, in fact some days the cakes were only just cool from the oven when they went on sale. But I wanted to introduce something different that told the customers that there was something new and a little different going on at the Georgian Tearooms. I tried to dream up a special idea and came up with a good one.

We decided to put on a Sunday Brunch menu that tilted towards the Victorian era. Our menu was built around dishes such as kedgeree and devilled kidneys, black pudding on salad with pine nuts, and bagels with cream cheese and smoked salmon, with boozy whisky porridge (courtesy of John Tovey and Miller Howe) or hot winter fruits and crème fraiche, to start. The new Sunday menu was popular and word started to go around that we were different from the usual café in Leeds. This Sunday Brunch, together with our real homemade scones and cakes, plus the fact that all of our sandwiches and meals were made to order, seemed to please people who were looking for something other than the branches of café chains that were beginning to open all over Leeds.

I suppose one of the most satisfying aspects of the tearoom was that Richard was working well and gaining in confidence so much, as we coped together with the business of serving our customers. In all the time we were there he never had a day off other than if he was lost in cold or something similar. Rarely did we argue other than the usual raised voices occasionally if some order was missed – the kind of shouting that happens in every kitchen when things need to be speeded up. He really was blossoming from the experience. However I realised that we were only just scraping through money-wise, mainly because I was employing youngsters on Saturdays and Sundays, and some weeks trade suddenly dipped if the weather was bad and of course staff still had to be paid. There were mornings when we did not have a customer until after twelve o'clock. So I soon recognised that I was not going to get rich on the café's income.

In order to boost the takings a little I tried to open up for a couple of evenings a week, hoping to produce a set menu for a three course inclusive dinner menu, perhaps even themed evenings with music from young opera friends. But the owners of the antique floors below us would not go along with these late openings, so that idea came to nothing. We tried to add one or two outdoor summer tables, near the entrance to the building, even though the logistics of running up and down the back stairs was a nightmare, but health and safety declared that we needed a new downstairs preparation area if we wanted to carry on, and that was impossible. Another idea was to invite a pianist to play for a couple of hours every Friday afternoon after the lunch trade had ended. David, the repetiteur from Opera Group fitted the bill admirably, and he happily arrived with his keyboard, set up in one corner of the café and played Ivor Novello tunes and Strauss waltzes to our afternoon tea customers. But that didn't bring in any extra customers either, and even though I really enjoyed singing along with him if we were without customers, and polishing up my own operatic repertoire for a change, I eventually had to call it a day as it was costing more than it added to the takings.

Soon in order to keep things going at all I reluctantly started to do recruitment work again as I had been approached by a Manchester company, a former competitor of mine in the recruitment field. I joined them two days a week and found a young man to take over my place in the kitchen for those days. We were better off financially that way but it meant I was working seven days a week now, doing the busiest days at the tearooms, and haring off to Manchester for two days as well as visiting new work clients all over the UK. I suppose something had to give and when I found out that the building's owners, where we were, had sold the building for re-development, without any consultation or thought for the lease-holders, that was the last straw. I had spent probably twenty thousand pounds in total, acquiring the business, and renewing carpets, fittings, and generally improving things. Now we were to be out within the year and no compensation. We decided to cut our losses and go immediately, which was a very sad decision. I joined the Manchester outfit full-time and Richard tried to find work elsewhere. The year working in the tearooms had given him some good experience, but working in a big commercial kitchen was very different, and taking the loud shouting from strangers was just too much for him. Sadly he has never found anything remotely as suitable since.

12

Roving the
UK

Prospect Hill Hotel

Kirkoswald · in the Eden Valley

Telephone Lazonby 500 STD 076883

The Old Byre Bar

M. B... of 4 ....
date 1/10/83 ....

Champagne £28.50

£

I.& J.M.Henderson · VAT Reg No.257426937

108

When my partner John and I met in 1995, I had no idea that I was about to begin the "good years" of my life. Oh there had been some good periods before – the birth of my children to name but three, but partnership-wise I had not found the right person with whom I could spend the rest of my life, and had a lot of hurt, guilt and sadness behind me as a result. I had been alone for more than two years, and working away in the tearooms with Richard, and although my staunch group of friends had always included me in every social gathering that happened, I still felt like half a couple when we were all together. I had no other places to go socially where I was viewed as a woman who happened to be alone but getting on with life. In short I knew I had reached the point where I was ready to make new friends.

My birthday was coming up in May so I decided to treat myself and buy membership into a dining out club, a version of Singles Groups that was becoming quite popular in the nineties. I posted off my details with an accompanying cheque, and duly received a programme of events, mainly details of which restaurant was chosen on which night and an invitation to join the people going along. I looked down the list and opted to jump in with an evening at Korks Bistro in Otley about a week later. As I expected when the actual day arrived I wondered what on earth had possessed me. Nevertheless I got myself done up, stepped into my car and drove to Otley. When I went into the bar where the group were gathered my first impression was of a lively set of about twenty people, mixed ages and roughly speaking half and half men and women which was a bit of a surprise as usually these clubs have far more female members than male. Someone recognised I was new and drew me into their conversation. I bought myself a drink so that I had something to hold on to and after a bit of chat it was signalled that we could go through to the restaurant.

As near as was possible everyone sat down in a "man woman man woman" arrangement and I found myself between two chaps who were both pleasant. John was the guy on my right and as we chatted I discovered that he was a single man, younger than I was, had never been married and had spent probably twenty years or more travelling and working overseas. He was lively and very interesting to talk to and having quickly established that my other neighbour thought of himself as God's gift to women, I carried on talking to John. The practice at these evenings was that after each course the men would move up a couple of places so that everyone met and chatted to the maximum number of members in an evening. As we were almost at the end of the table, when the move came it meant he moved around the corner and ended up opposite to me so we still had the chance to go on talking. I can remember that he was surprised when I said that I was not looking for a partner but it would be good to meet someone who would be happy to go to the theatre occasionally or even to a restaurant together. Apparently most of the divorcees were desperately looking for the next husband or at the very least, someone to lean on. The evening ended and I went home thinking that it had been a pleasant change, pleased that I had made the effort, and I would definitely go to other such events. In fact I went to several restaurant meals but did not come across John again until early September when we both opted to go to an evening at Bingley Arms, at Bardsey. He remembered our previous meeting and when we moved to sit down I was pleased to find he took the place next to me, which I realised was a love-seat for two – must have been an omen! We talked non-stop throughout the three courses of the meal again and he surprised everyone by declaring between courses that he would not be moving round that evening as the guests normally used to do. From the brief surprised silence that followed his announcement, it seemed that nobody had bucked the trend before.

To cut a long story short, we did agree to try a meal out together, off the club programme, and that first meal was at "The Angel" at Hetton, near Skipton. I well remember that John called for me at my home at seven, we drove to Hetton, shared a lovely meal, came back home and I eventually suggested he should go at around three in the morning, and we had never stopped talking for a minute! I cannot remember what we ate but I do recall that we ordered a bottle of Fleurie, which became "our wine" for later significant anniversaries and celebrations. This "evening out at a decent restaurant" was repeated a few times and by Christmas we both regarded our friendship as promising I think. So I suppose it proves that when you are not looking and least expect to find someone that is when it will happen.

As we grew towards being a couple, we started to go on little offs to places in England and Wales that we both fancied seeing and so began to store up lots of shared

111

memories. These weekend trips continued after we started to live together in May 1996 and we have many happy memories to draw on. The first weekend we spent together had its moments – some of them very private and memorable, some of them almost embarrassing. I recall that as John had booked the hotel, a small private hotel in Kirkoswald, in the Lake District, I decided to add a special touch by phoning ahead and ordering a bottle of champagne to be in our room as we arrived. We found the bottle on the bedroom side table when we arrived, opened it and celebrated the start of the weekend with a glass of champagne in our room before dinner, but when we returned after dinner the beds were turned down and the half bottle of champagne had been removed. I suppose that they thought that if it was no longer chilled it was not required and perhaps might not be suitable for drinking, but at £29.50 a bottle I was a bit miffed. The embarrassing moment was next morning, our first breakfast together in an hotel, when we entered the dining room and realised from the geography of the room that it was directly underneath our bedroom and all seated there had probably been privilege to any creaking from the bed overhead. What made matters worse was that as our coffee arrived I said to John "Do you take sugar in coffee?" and as soon as the words were out of my mouth, realized I had confirmed the thoughts of all the other guests who had decided we were there on a "dirty week-end".

After that first weekend away we visited Norfolk to stay at a small place in Wells next the Sea where we both remember that we had to order dinner in the morning before we left for the day, and that the owner kept emphasising that whatever we ordered she would serve it with at least five accompanying vegetables! Next Spring, in Aberystwyth we found ourselves in a small bed and breakfast establishment, miles from anywhere with the continuous background baa-ing noise of young lambs in the next field, keeping us from sleeping 'til the early hours, and then waking us very early just after we had at last managed to drop off to sleep. We had a rather uneventful short break in Bury St Edmunds, Suffolk but then followed it up with a memorable stay at a posh hotel, the De Vere Hotel, Slaley Hall, in Northumberland. The young waiter who served us at dinner was horrified when we managed to set fire to the beautiful white damask tablecloth by knocking over the lighted candle he placed at our table. Food seemed secondary on that particular evening.

I had by this time joined in an organisation named Holiday Property Bond, a way of buying into a holiday ownership scheme resembling time-share in some ways, but with the main difference that we could go to any of the properties at any time, rather than being tied to the same week at the same resort every year. One of our first UK trips was to the county of Pembrokeshire where the property was a stunning castle on the cliffs at St Brides. We drove through Shropshire and then into Wales choosing a route that would take us past "The Walnut Tree" a famous food pub near Abergavenny that had a long established reputation of its Italian chef/proprietor Franco Taruscio, and his amazing food, and a place that I had always wanted to visit. Their reputation was for fabulous food cooked with very local ingredients such as the delicious Welsh lamb, cooked with an Italian twist. I learned recently that it was a favourite too with Elizabeth David, my all-time favourite food writer. Unfortunately we chose to lunch there just as there was a change of ownership after thirty years, and found that they had created a new extension to the pub that seemed totally soulless and without atmosphere, and food that bordered on being OK but at grossly inflated prices. It was a very disappointing start to the week.

However the week did brighten up gastronomically speaking when we paid a visit to a country restaurant that was in all the "recommended" guides at the time. It seems to have disappeared these days and in fact on the day we went there we arrived quite late at lunchtime as it took us so long to find it. I think it was called Anne's Farmhouse Kitchen and was part of a beautiful old working farm. We got there to find we were the only lunch-time diners, but also expected that day was a team from a local radio station who were going to interview the proprietor about her interest in regional cheeses. If I were asked to describe the style of her cooking I would call it "farmhouse abundance" as every plate she set before us was loaded with wonderful food in enormous portions. John had ordered what used to be one of his favourite starters, fish soup. This item can vary so much from restaurant to restaurant, some preferring the chunky, full of fish version, while others serve a more concentrated smooth soup with accompaniments of grated cheese, croutons, and rouille (a type of herb and garlic mayonnaise). Here the soup was chunky just as John preferred it but the surprise was that it came to the table in a tureen filled to the top, and just for him. After he had gorged himself on that while I ate my less substantial but nevertheless good paté, we both waited for our main course, a rabbit casserole. We both love rabbit but we were knocked out when a whole rabbit arrived at the table in a deep rich sauce – again just for the two of us – and accompanied by so many vegetables. We did our best but even John was struggling to finish.

Finally when we could eat no more Anne came to us and told us that in view of this impending broadcast she had prepared a cheese board for the journalist to describe but we were welcome to sample it too. We agreed and found ourselves faced with an enormous selection on a board as big as the next-door table for two. There was every local cheese that could be sourced from the area, with Welsh butter and home-made biscuits. On any other occasion we could have dined happily just from this cheese-board alone, but after the meal we had just eaten all we could do was nibble at one or two of the most irresistible. When we next visited St Brides we tried to find the restaurant again but apparently it's no longer there. What a pity. It was unforgettable.

Another memorable weekend was a visit to Bath, a city I had never previously visited. We usually found our places to stay by using a little guide called "Staying Off The Beaten Track" and this place was typical, down at the end of several winding roads and quite rural other than a couple of neighbouring houses along the lane. The proprietor was quite effusive in her welcome and lost no time in telling us that she had been a runner up in the "landlady of the year" competition. We had a pleasant room, other than it had no lock on the door and no en-suite bathroom. However it was only for a couple of nights so we accepted it. We had a drive into Bath, visited the old Roman Baths and Museum, found somewhere to eat that was not particularly memorable, (in fact John sent his fish soup back as it was so awful) then returned to the B&B and retired for the night.

Next morning, the minute we set foot out of our room, our hostess appeared at the bottom of the stairs ready to show us into the dining room. By the end of the weekend

I imagined that she must live under the stairs as we never could manage to leave our room without her appearing instantly in the hallway ready to have a word with us. However on this first morning, she waited until we were sitting at a table then detailed all the items available for breakfast. Then with a flourish and gesture towards a gingham-lidded jar taking pride of place on the table, she said, "And let me introduce you to the marmalade". Never have I had to control myself as much as that moment as I knew I did not dare look at John for fear of laughing out loud. She then took down our breakfast choices and shouted, "Go, Fen!" to her husband, who was standing by ready to cook in the kitchen. We completed our stay there without further event but we still always say "Let me introduce you to the marmalade", whenever we open a new jar of the stuff at home.

13

Always Follow the Workmen

Salad du Geziers

(Duck Gizzard Salad)

It is unlikely that in England you will be able to obtain duck gizzards, if you do manage to get them (2 should be enough) then chop them into small pieces and fry quickly in a non-stick pan.

My alternative would be to use a duck breast, seared on both sides so that the centre meat remains pink, leave to cool slightly while you fry a couple of rashers of bacon in the duck fat that the breast should have produced, then slice both bacon and duck breast into pieces and toss onto dressed salad leaves.

1995 and as I packed the last of my removal boxes ready to leave the big detached house on Beeston Road in South Leeds, I had many memories to take with me to the next phase of my life. Some were good and some were not. Ten years before I had set up my business there, the Maggie Poppa Consultancy, built offices to house it as it grew, and it had been a roaring success. In the office extension next to the house, after we moved the business to other premises, the space being somewhat unusual, it became a space for entertaining, and it was the scene of many wonderful fundraising dinners. It was there that I celebrated my fiftieth birthday with a huge party for friends and family, but then disgraced myself with a bottle of gin and being quite drunk by ten o'clock, had to be put to bed. However, that was all behind me, the ten year relationship that lasted whilst I lived there was over, and two years on, I had sold my house. And even though there was a last minute hiccup when the promised cheque did not materialise at the signing-off day, my trust in the buyer had paid off and when I got back from holiday, the money was in my bank account. The big decision had been made about where to live next and I had eventually accepted the offer from my new partner, John, to move in with him. Scurrying round with only six weeks to find and buy a house seemed to be totally the wrong thing to do.

If I was not immediately going to need my capital, I decided that I might spend a little of it. For a few years I had been considering investment in a holiday home ownership scheme that would provide top class self-catering holidays for the rest of my life. I had experienced too many do-it-yourself holidays when we arrived at the hired flat or cottage, and found that the rooms were filled with second-hand furniture, bed-linen was often dubious in colour and texture, and the kitchen cupboards were stocked with a complete set of non-matching crockery and glasses courtesy of the nearest jumble sale. My inspection of the nearest site of the holiday organisation at Rosedale Abbey in North Yorkshire had proved that this was definitely not the case with them. Their kitchen cupboards were stacked with good quality dishes, glasses and plates, the thread count on the bed-linen was the highest available, and had an inviting silky texture. I decided that this was the moment to plunge, and after I had parted with my first cash investment the transactions were signed on the dotted line, and I was free to pore over the pages of their glossy brochure choosing where our first foray could be.

The choice was France. I could choose from either St Simeon in the Paris region, Manoir d'Hilguy in Brittany, or a spot in the Dordogne called Constant. It was the architecture of the latter area which attracted me as Constant was a hamlet, rebuilt in traditional Perigord style, and was close enough to Bergerac to provide a glimpse of town life should we need it. So we duly requested a cottage for two people, packed the cases and loaded the car. These days there are small airports across the Dordogne that allow holiday-makers to fly there directly and then hire a car for the holiday. But on that first trip we decided to take our own vehicle, drive to the car ferry and then onwards down through the French countryside. It's a long drive down to the Dordogne so we decided on an overnight stop in Rouen, not a very successful one I must admit. Some of the chains of cheap hotels that have spawned branches all across the UK have come from France. The Nova Hotels, Ibex and the Campanile chains are all French and we chose a branch of the latter for our overnight stop. One of the reasons these chain hotels are cheap is that they are often in less than picturesque sites. This was no exception, as we had to drive through a gloomy and largely uninteresting industrial estate to reach it. So not much of a view from the window of the tiny chalet room we were allocated. There are no frills at this price, just a wardrobe, flower-fabric covered bed and an ensuite bathroom. Breakfast was basic and adequate but didn't deserve a better description. So we pushed on to Constant.

Arriving at the holiday village we saw clusters of character-laden brick built old cottages all with the quaintly shaped roofs typical of the area. It looked welcoming and bright. We found our home for the week to be all that we expected with stylish, tip-top dark red furnishings in the lounge, gleaming modern kitchen, and here and there, exposed stone walls. The unpacking completed, our thoughts turned to food as always, so having bought the basics for the larder and the fridge on the way down, decided that a late lunch was in order.

Our policy when eating abroad has always been to search out where the local traders and workpeople are eating their mid-day meal rather than make for the obvious tourist spots. We have rarely if ever been disappointed by what was on offer. I can well remember this particular day near Constant when we drew up at the first café stop we came to that displayed the usual " menu du jour" outside the premises. This obligatory menu designed to provide good value local food for the local workforce is ideal if one wants to try the real food of the country rather than the tourist-aimed, Anglicised versions. On this particular day the menu showed several no-frills choices most of which we could translate and have a fair idea of what would arrive on our plates. We went in. Needless to say if you pursue this policy of visiting what sometimes can be described as truck-stops, then you are often the only tourist in the place, and usually dressed in holiday garb, so you have to put up with the stares from their regular clientele. But we are used to that and it's usually jovial company with workmen eating and loudly discussing the news of the day, rather than the hushed tones of a British café.

As we sat down we tried to get to grips with the menu, bearing in mind that for both of us, our French had been acquired at grammar school many years ago, and only occasionally brought out and dusted down every few years when holidaying in France. However we could translate all the dishes on the menu except for "salade du geziers de canard". We knew the last word translated as duck, but what bit of the duck? Not knowing doesn't usually deter us though, so we ordered that dish as a starter. It arrived looking like small pieces of roasted meat on a well-dressed green salad. It was tasty but for me a bit gristly and chewy, although John enjoyed it very much. We proceeded to the second course of sliced meat followed by the customary salad, and then to pudding, a small piece of fruit tart. Both were well-cooked courses and we left feeling sated and satisfied. When we got back to Constant we called at reception and used the French-English dictionary to see what we had just eaten. It was duck's gizzards! We should have known that I suppose, in an area that produces fois gras and therefore presumably has plenty of those particular bits of the ducks' anatomy going spare. I don't eat foie gras because I'm not happy about the process that geese go through, and since that day I haven't eaten "salade du geziers" either!

However following the workmen into small cafes has remained the policy that we adopt as we want to have good, typically local food, and there are a couple of instances where we had wonderful meals as a result. In Majorca we found ourselves in a back street restaurant with a huge dining room, looking almost like a canteen, with dozens of tables with white linen cloths. It was filled with lots of local shop and office workers, there was no written menu, and after a waitress rattled off what was available that day, we jumped in where we could. Again, it was a wonderful meal starting with a rice dish, followed by roast chicken and salad, and fresh fruit to follow. We returned several times that week always to a different good-value menu.

Perhaps the most memorable was in Florence, when we started to feel hungry after walking round the tourist attractions all morning, and it was hot and humid too. I needed to sit down and eat. I spied some street workmen down tools and look as if they were preparing to take a break. We watched where they went but they seemed to disappear into a hole in the wall. Then just as we were about to give up and look elsewhere, a group of smartly uniformed pilots from Alitalia arrived in their dark blue jackets banded with gold braid on the sleeves. They too stepped into the void. Looking more closely there was a narrow door, unmarked, but nothing saying this was a restaurant. Curiosity had got the better of us by now, and we pushed open the door to follow. It was a fairly small white-washed room but it was packed with people all sitting on benches at long tables, and loud with chatter. The form seemed to be that you took a place on one of the benches near the door, and as the meal progressed everyone moved up a little as people left, and any newcomers took the newly-vacated spaces nearest to the door. Here again there was no printed menu, but instead an elderly waitress rattled off in local dialect what was available, and even though I speak Italian well, I needed to hear the list a couple of times before I could grasp a few words. It seemed better (if a little rude) to point at what someone was being served and say, "I'll have one of those". We started with a robust local recipe, vegetable soup-cum-stew, followed by an escalope of meat which could have been veal, pork or beef served with a smooth and flavoursome cream sauce, a side salad and then a freshly made tart of local strawberries to complete the meal. All for something like eight pounds (about thirteen euros then) and that included good bread, local red wine and water.

I think many people would have been put off by the Faulty Towers-like cooking routines in that café. Certainly the local Environmental Health had not been round and done an inspection in the recent weeks. The tall, wiry, middle-aged chef cooked in a tiny space perhaps six foot square, where food in different stages of preparation was piled everywhere, dishes of pasta on open shelves, plates of cooked meat on the highest shelf, and best of all every ten minutes or so the chef himself lit a cigarette and smoked while he worked, presumably with ash falling anywhere beneath. But if you were largely undeterred by these practices, and everyone around us seemed to find it acceptable, then the food was incredibly good and very cheap.

We took the view that if a team from Alitalia were happy to make a trip from the airport into the city centre to eat here, then we were up for it too. As we moved up a place each time between courses, the whole meal took less than an hour and by that time we had gradually moved down the benches to the far end which meant that our time was up and we should pay and vacate. The total hardly made a dent in our spending money and we left feeling most satisfied. The trouble is we could never find the place again in a million years if we revisited Florence. That seems to be the same situation with all the similar places we find. Wonderful food, memorable experiences, but then they disappear from the map, and the next time we start again and search out another prospect with that curious faith that we shall have wonderful food even if we don't always know what we are eating.

14

Roving the
World

New York's Dry Martini

The recommended proportions for this classic cocktail is

3 parts gin
½ part extra dry vermouth
(white martini)
ice cubes.
Cocktail olive

Put ice cubes in glass, (the traditional y-shaped martini glass is ideal), pour gin and vermouth into a cocktail shaker, shake well and pour over the ice cubes. Add the olive on a cocktail stick.

A good tip is that the better the gin, the better the martini!

John has always been wonderful at planning surprise trips for me for my birthday. He's booked short trips to Majorca, Iceland, Barcelona, Prague, and one year a balloon flight over Yorkshire complete with champagne. In 1998 he had chosen a few days in Rome that turned out to be a memorable trip in many ways. Perhaps the most memorable was sitting one lunchtime in an *enoteca* – a sort of street-corner bar with light snacks – where there were barrels of different local new-season wines made from various fruits such as peaches, strawberries, and apricots. Trying one glass led to another and another and it's one of the few times I have seen John tipsy. I don't remember walking back to our hotel fifty yards away, but I know that suddenly it was seven o'clock in the evening and I had a thumping head, but if asked I would do it again!

So for John's birthday the following September I decided that I would try to arrange something really unusual and seeing that I was then earning well as I was working in Manchester managing the manufacturing recruitment side of Star Executives, I thought I could afford a trip further a field. Passing a travel agent's window one lunchtime, on my way back to the office, I spotted an inclusive trip to New York and decided that was it. I spent lunchtime the next day sitting in their office tying up all the loose ends. With these birthday surprises it has always been our choice for the person being surprised to not know where he or she is going until reaching the airport, so I packed our cases, planned the rail journey to the Manchester air terminal and waited for the look of surprise on John's face when he finally realised our destination. Well there was a look of real surprise perhaps even shock, as our trips had previously been within the boundaries of Europe. He had obviously thought we were going elsewhere.

But when we arrived and were taken by limousine to our hotel, The Loews Hotel in Manhattan, slowly the smiles on both our faces widened. We had neither of us been to New York before, in fact for me this was my first US visit, and it was hard to know where to look. Everything seemed so familiar largely due to films and TV series that had been viewed over the years. Looking up you could see all the skyscrapers, looking down were the pavements with inlaid commemorative stones in some instances, looking around brought the wonderful store windows into view, and everywhere there were famous sights to be spotted. It was so exciting. After unpacking we decided that our top of the list to start off the evening was to go down to the bar, climb up onto the bar stools and order dry martinis. Nobody does a dry martini like a New York bartender, so we sat there feeling worldly and excited, sipping very dry martinis and elegantly swishing around the green olive.

The three days were packed full with such a thrilling programme. I had spared no expense so as well as the limousines, I had booked a theatre trip to see "Cats" on Broadway, and an excursion to Harlem on the Sunday morning, first touring the familiar-looking brownstone buildings on the famous streets of the neighbourhood, before being guests at a gospel service in a local church. The singing (and dancing) was amazing and the choir's sound was very moving. We left the church feeling totally uplifted and were then whisked off to lunch at what had been described simply as " a famous venue". We were both more than surprised when the coach pulled into the car park of "The Cotton Club" and we walked in to find a live jazz combo already up and running, ready to play to us while we grazed on a breathtaking Creole-style buffet lunch which featured dishes of jambalaya (the Creole version of paella), more shrimp and crawfish recipes, rice and red beans, and everything spiced and peppery. John certainly couldn't tackle that menu now. Just being there in the actual Cotton Club was wonderful and typical of everything that happened in New York. Wherever you are, you have always seen a film in that setting and feel as if you are walking into a familiar film set. People say that it's dirty and sometimes dangerous, but in all the time we were there I never felt nervous, we found the streets were so clean, and yellow cabs actually slowed at amber traffic lights and obeyed the traffic signals, unlike our own cabbies who shoot through lights at red on a regular basis.

While we were in New York we were able to copy other Americanisms that we'd always wanted to try. Ordering "pastrami on rye to go, and hold the mayo" in the local delicatessen as if we did this everyday; eating pancakes and syrup for breakfast in a street corner diner; and cutting into the largest, juiciest t-bone steak we'd ever seen in a little restaurant in Greenwich village. It was a wonderful trip which we did say that we would repeat, but as yet we've not got round to it. The short stay was brought to an ideal end by a stretch limousine pulling up at our hotel to take us to the airport, and my first experience of sitting ten yards away from the chauffeur who looked like a personal guard he was so broad, but he chatted away happily until we reached JFK airport. Brilliant!

But we hadn't finished travelling that year for we had been planning our "trip of a lifetime" during the summer. John has travelled all over the world from the age of eighteen when he was on his university course sponsored by United Nations and sent off to the West Africa and the Far East to work on UN projects, to years later when, in his twenties, he roved around alone behind the iron curtain just wanting to see as much as possible of how people in other countries existed. But the one place he had never managed to see and had a great longing to visit was New Zealand. In fact had we not met when we did he would probably have applied to emigrate out there. So we started planning a trip that would span more than a month, starting in November when the temperature would just be warming up nicely. In 1998 there was still a very good independent travel agent in Leeds where we found a specialist on New Zealand who had travelled both islands several times himself and could offer us the benefit of his experience. What we wanted to do was go there independently rather than be part of an organised party, and tour both North and South islands doing a combination of car driving, rail journeys and some necessary boat trips. We read up the travel guides, compiled our possible route, and then with this chap's help booked our travel programme for the month including a couple of days stopping in Hong Kong and on the return journey, a stopover in Fiji.

We boarded the Singapore Airlines aeroplane at London Heathrow, after the short connecting flight from Leeds, and immediately the serene, beautifully dressed flight attendants put everyone at ease. I am not a confident flyer and I make myself fly to save time more than to enjoy it, but these young women were wonderful and I had a very pleasant flight, courtesy of their team. At each meal we were presented with a printed menu of real food which also came up to par when we tasted it, and the twelve or so hours to Hong Kong passed without problems. We were staying at a hotel near the waterfront and not in too busy an area. I did enjoy the trip over the bay to Hong Kong Island even though the Star Ferry sat too low in the water for my liking. I also enjoyed having a drink on a balcony at the complex on The Peak, but in general Hong Kong was not my kind of place. Too busy and loud, interesting but I had no inclination to return. My one attempt at *dimsum* was not a spectacular success and whenever I have eaten Chinese food I always feel that I chose the wrong dish, and what was being eaten at the next table would have been much better.

For the next leg of the journey we switched to Quantas Airlines, and found the flight girls there were of a different breed. Still providing good service, but in terms of looking smart and attractive, they were light years behind the Singapore team with a very dated style of uniform including hats that were more appropriate for church on Sundays. However again a good flight and before long we were flying low over the miles of golden beach that was the strand on the topmost part of North Island. After landing we collected luggage, then our car, and set off on our first New Zealand driving stretch. We were aiming to get from Auckland where we had landed to Paihia in the Bay of Islands for our first overnight and as there is little traffic on the roads after leaving the city, it was achievable. We were staying in a hotel where, as most of these hotels seemed to have, we were given a room that also had a kitchen attached but for our first night we opted to eat out. We asked around, and were directed to a new restaurant that specialised in fish. When we found it, it seemed very busy, and the lady who greeted us was going to turn us away but we pleaded "that this was the only night here, we had heard so much about it" etc and soon she had managed to squeeze us into a corner. The food was sublime, light seafood starters, grilled fish that I think was as near to bream as any other fish I'd seen, and lovely smooth New Zealand Sauvignon wine. I hoped that this was going to be typical of the food we would find in New Zealand, and indeed it was.

Over the next two weeks we drove or train-ed and zig-zagged our way from the tip of North Island to the very southernmost part of South Island and enjoyed every minute of it. Restaurants were not only serving wonderful fresh food with very modern takes on traditional style dishes but the staff who brought us the food were so friendly and good at their jobs; nothing like the largely untrained and often discourteous staff to be found all over the UK. We remember one typical example of good service while we were staying in Christchurch. We had left our hotel in the main square and wandered down to the information and booking office just yards away to try to get ourselves to a coastal town we'd heard about that was largely French-speaking. When we asked for the time that the bus left the answer was "Oh dear, it left about five minutes ago. But hang on here and I'll see if I can call him and get him to come back for you." We were amazed that she thought this would be possible and in fact she couldn't reach the driver, but undeterred, she then rang the bus company, told them about us, and we were told that someone would come and pick us up and then we would hare after the bus until we caught it up. That seemed to be wonderful service but our mouths dropped open when a BMW saloon drew up and the MD of the company himself told us to hop in and he'd take us. He chatted happily to us and we discovered he had done his University studying in Leeds where we came from, and after 45 minutes we managed to catch the coach when he told us to wait by this roadside coffee shop, have ourselves a muffin and coffee, and the coach would be with us in minutes. Indeed it was and they would take no more than the usual fare for their trouble. Can you imagine anyone in the UK doing that?

Mentioning muffins, that was definitely one of our super discoveries in New Zealand. Every bakery and corner store produces fresh-baked muffins in the mornings, and what variety. Our favourite was definitely the crumbly muffin that held blueberries and ice cream in the middle. How they managed to keep frozen ice cream in the middle of a muffin fresh from the oven, I never did find out but it was superb. We had wonderful meals in Queenstown and Wellington, but unfortunately I did not keep the menus to remind me of what we ate. New Zealand was a charming and beautiful country and again we have every intention of re-visiting, but so far we have not done that trip either.

Fiji for me was quite a disaster as it was so hot (40 degrees in the shade) that I stayed under my umbrella asleep all day, catching up as I had laid awake all night watching the geckos and lizards racing across the walls of our log cabin and hoping that there were no snakes or spiders out there too. My unfulfilled travel wish would be to go to the rain forest to try to see gorillas but unfortunately I would not survive the fear of snakes and insects so that's a dream that will probably not come true. All I ate while I was on Fiji was fresh fruit as in that heat I had no appetite, but one evening when it cooled a little we did venture down to the bar and I recall being invited to drink a very suspicious looking drink by some local people. I never did find out what was in it but I slept like a log that night, so who knows!

15

Le Manoir aux Quat' Saisons

Notre Menu Gourmand

RAYMOND BLANC'S "MENU GOURMAND" GIVES THE
OPPORTUNITY OF SAMPLING A SELECTION OF
SEASONAL SPECIALITIES.
FOR THE WHOLE TABLE ONLY

Appetiser plate

****

Marinated red mullet,

orange and lemon vinaigrette with coriander, red pepper jus

****

Medley of green asparagus spears and girolles

****

Pan-fried seabass and artichoke poivrade ;

basil oil and raw tomato coulis

****

Roasted fillet of milk-fed veal in its own juices;

rosemary macaroni

****

Rhubarb and strawberry soup

****

Pistachio soufflé with a bitter cocoa sorbet

****

Café "Pur Arabica", petits fours et chocolats du Manoir

****

(£84)

****

Cheese may be taken as an extra course (£9)

****

Les Spécialités d'été

Starters

Main courses

Suprême de canette de Barbarie, sauce au vieux vinaigre de balsamique et tamarin	Roasted breast of Barbary duck with an aged Modena vinegar and tamarind sauce £32
Escalope de loup de mer poêlée et grosse langoustine rôtie, huile vierge au basilic	Pan-fried seabass fillet and roasted langoustine; basil oil and raw tomato coulis £32

The millennium was approaching, and all manner of madness was around. For example, we had toyed with the idea of going to Edinburgh for the experience of a true Hogmanay to celebrate the passing of 1999, but when we approached the prestigious Balmoral Hotel with its wonderful view of the Royal Mile, we were told that at this stage, names were being taken and a detailed package would be announced at a later date. In fact what was happening was that all the hotels were waiting to see how the market demand panned out before letting it be known what their own charge would be. Sure enough, early Autumn we received a provisional programme (in other words the exact entertainment was as yet unspecified) but the price of the five-day package had now been set. Guessing at the level of that figure would leave you miles away from the reality, I'm sure. In fact they proposed charging a minimum of £4000 per person − £800 per day − for this period. We spent a few amusing hours trying to imagine what we would eat or drink that would amount to £800 of value for each day. Needless to say we declined the invitation. Instead we accepted an invitation to a "dress-up-to-the-nines" dinner to be held on New Year's Eve at the house of opera group friends, Steve and Christina. It was a truly wonderful evening as Christina is also a fabulous cook, and it was rounded off with fireworks in the garden, still a novelty at the millennium.

However I had decided that as I had had the good fortune to find the right partner at last, and we had reached such a momentous point of starting a new millennium, I would try and get myself in shape to hopefully ensure that I would be around to see as much of the twenty-first century as possible. In other words some of my accrued weight had to come off. At five foot ten inches tall I had always been a large lady and was quite used to people saying "well you're tall you can carry it" and "but you always look so nice, you hide it very well". All were comments designed to make me feel better but did not always work. The main reason for taking the decision though was that I felt it was time. Every woman who has dieted knows that there are times when you can, and times when you can't; it's all a matter of being committed. I opted to join one of the well-known slimming clubs, Slimming World, and went off to my first meeting without telling anyone my intentions. I thought it was better to do that rather than start and fail and have my friends realise that I'd failed. But surprisingly I took to it like a duck to water and from losing four pounds in my first week went from strength to strength. I knew I was aiming to get to approximately four or five stone lower than my starting weight so as an incentive, John suggested that when I had lost my first two stones of weight, approximately half way, he would take me to lunch at Raymond Blanc's famous Le Manoir aux Quat'Saisons in Oxfordshire, the restaurant I had always placed at the top of my wish list. It may sound strange celebrating losing weight by going out for a gourmet meal, but in my experience really fine food is never filling, outfacing and super-high in calories, but instead is based on simply wonderful flavours from good ingredients and awesome technical expertise. It was something to aim for indeed.

At that time, Slimming World advocated eating lots of food from either a red or green plan (mainly protein or mainly vegetables) and the fact that I did not have to starve myself seemed to work well and I achieved a steady weight loss. Even though I had never suffered from a lack of confidence because of being overweight, it did make me feel much better in many ways as the pounds came off. Because I was successful and also perhaps the type of person they often liked to run their classes, I was approached to see whether I would like to start to train as a class consultant. I decided to try my hand at it and after the training spent almost three years very happily helping other people, both men and women, to achieve their own weight goals. It was a very enjoyable job to have as you are privileged to see how a personality changes and confidence starts to blossom as the weight comes off. In general most people are happier when they achieve the weight loss they are aiming for, not to emulate skinny models or anything of that order, but simply to feel better about themselves.

By early May that first year I had lost my first two stone, so as promised John started to make arrangements for us to visit Le Manoir. We were to go in late June and stop for lunch at the restaurant before continuing on to a village in the Cotswolds to stay for a couple of days. It sounded idyllic and my dream of seeing Raymond Blanc's gastronomic palace was titillating my taste buds.

When we arrived at the restaurant, a concierge met us and walked us through the front gardens to the main entrance. He was typical of all the staff we met – pleasant, unstuffy and welcoming. We were shown to one of several light and airy drawing rooms filled with super comfortable settees and armchairs, where we sat and looked over the menus for the day, and sipped our pre-lunch drinks. We were quite aware before we arrived that there was on offer a set lunch menu and an a la carte, and as there was a marked difference in price we had agreed to select the set menu. However, once we were seated and started to look at the comparatively simple set menu, against the delights on offer on the a la carte, our resolve wavered, and we decided eventually to go for it and order exactly what we wanted and damn the cost! After all this was a special occasion.

We both opted to skip starters and go straight to a main course and then look forward to a pudding or cheese, and I think we made the right choice. We were shown into the dining room again an impressive light and airy space, to a large round table where we faced into the room and could see all that was happening. The tables gleamed with fresh linen, polished silverware, and shining glassware. I always enjoy people watching but here the delight was watching the service, and it was impeccable. Well-trained staff glided to and fro, and were attentive but never overly so. Our *amuse geule* (pre-starter) arrived – a delicious small portion of soup served in a coffee cup and saucer, and we were pleased that we had not ordered a starter. At first glance this small cup of soup, announced as "essence of tomato" seemed rather weak and colourless. But from the first sip there was a flavour burst of tomato in the mouth that was phenomenal.

After that pleasant opening to the meal our chosen dishes arrived. I had ordered the suckling pig described on the menu as "Spit roasted best end or saddle of suckling pig with a marjoram scented jus". It looked wonderful, a picture on a plate, and it tasted every bit as good as it appeared. But when the cover was lifted from John's meal we both looked at each other in amazement, as the presentation of his meal was so beautiful. John had ordered rabbit described as "Braised shoulder of rabbit in a Pinot Noir red wine sauce; roasted loin in a tarragon and mustard jus". What took our breath away was the way that the loin was served in tiny, one inch long, perfect chops of the rabbit loin, all arranged precisely around the border of the plate with the rest of the dish arranged beautifully within that border. The dishes on the menu were expensive but it was obvious where the costing went, as the dish was so labour intensive. They say that everyone eats with their eyes in the first seconds of seeing a dish, and we were certainly bowled over by the look of ours. Happily as we started to eat, the taste and flavour of the food was just as good as our first impression. We were in heaven.

Having consumed our main courses there was now a decision as to what we chose to follow. I had been watching fabulous pudding plates being delivered to other tables so I had already decided what I would have. My perfectly poached whole peach arrived in due course and both looked and tasted wonderful. At that time John was never a fan of puddings so he opted to have the cheese course, and there followed what was to become the most memorable part of our meal. For John's cheese, a designated cheese waiter arrived with a stunning selection of perhaps fifty cheeses beautifully arranged on a trolley. His knowledge of the range of cheeses was impressive, telling us the provenance of each product in front of him. John selected five different cheeses and small portions of each were placed in front of him complete with grapes, celery, nuts etc.

I drooled over the mouth-watering taste of my dessert. It was beautiful and neither too sweet nor too filling. John waxed lyrical about the quality of the cheeses and was very happy with his lot. In fact he enjoyed it so much he beckoned for the young cheese waiter and asked him quietly, "That was so good, does anyone ever ask for a second selection?" The waiter told him that he was welcome to have more and amazed us by recalling which five cheeses he had previously chosen and therefore which rather similar but different cheeses he would recommend. John began his second helping and declared them every bit as interesting and flavoursome as his first choice. We were both replete, but we opted to have coffee and petit fours at our table, so that we could linger a little longer and soak up as much atmosphere as possible in this wonderful establishment.

We were then invited to take a tour of the gardens while our bill was prepared, so we drifted out through another set of doors into the hedged kitchen garden where much of the vegetable produce used in the restaurant was grown. At that time very few chefs had started to grow their own herbs and vegetables, a practice which has become more popular in the last few years, but then it was a novelty. The gardener was on hand to answer any questions we had. We toured the gardens for a while then made our way back into the hotel to collect and pay our bill. John presented his card and paid and we didn't analyse any item until later. Then we found that as the waiter had confirmed that it was fine to have a second helping of cheese, so we had been charged for the second helping and at £17.00 per portion, John's cheese course had cost £34.00, about the amount that we would normally expect to cover a decent three course meal! Also, as a memento of the occasion I had asked for a copy of the menu to take away with me, and that also appeared as an item on the bill, at £8.00. But we were in such a good mood after our wonderful lunch that we opted not to quibble about either of these items as we did not want anything to mar the overwhelming memory of eating at Le Manoir aux Quat'Saisons.

16

Gordon Ramsay – Chelsea

Gordon Ramsay 15/8/03
Effusive staff. 10 waiters
etc for 30 covers. Over
patronising. m.B. Waters £4
Vichysoisse with langoustine
& caviar. Amuse.ge.
Signature dish Ravioli
of lobster a langoustine
with lemon + coriander
sauce. — Amu. £18.70
Foie gras terrine.
Cover of lamb on 8hr
cooked shoulder. Puree satisfy
Sweet caramelised shallots spinach
Roast Monkfish. Agony. Coffee
Baby squid. Sammy arbud ts.
Shared Tarte Tatin & chocd
Cardomom ?iccrea.
Pre-swirk Conette pana

A page from my note book.

August 2003, and my desire to eat in Britain's top restaurants was thriving. Top of the list so far had been Le Manoir au Quat' Saisons, Raymond Blanc's first-rate country house restaurant in Oxfordshire. But it had been three years since John had taken me there and I was itching to try one of the many famous London venues offering haute cuisine. As my daughter Anna lives in London and shares my love of good food (how could she not do, growing up with me) I thought a little trip to London including a posh lunch somewhere, would be just the job. I arranged a two-day trip down to the capital, reserving the second day to have lunch at Gordon Ramsay's Chelsea Restaurant. It was the middle of August and sultry weather had been forecast.

Obviously for restaurants at this level, booking just a couple of days before is not the best policy, unless you are a celebrity. These days their website advises booking a table at least two months in advance of your preferred luncheon date. But in 2003 Gordon Ramsay was still on the upward climb and had not yet reached the heights he has since achieved via his myriad TV programmes, so I thought it was worth trying. It paid off, apparently the glitterati were all out of town, and when I rang them I was told, "Yes madam we could offer you a table for two, but only at twelve noon I'm afraid". I took it, even though I knew that I would have to go without breakfast if I were to do justice to a good lunch as early in the day as that.

I travelled to London on the train the previous afternoon, spent a pleasant evening chatting to Anna over dinner at her home, then got up the next day looking forward to our lunchtime spree. In hot weather it's always difficult to decide what to wear. A compromise between looking smart and being comfortable in the heat has to be made, but finally I was ready. I had looked at the menu on their website so I knew roughly how much we would have to pay and mentally had decided that if we stuck to their table d'hote menu it was certainly affordable.

In the manner of most ordinary London inhabitants, and the fact that the distance was too far for a taxi ride, we took the tube to Chelsea and then had a fairly long, and for me, quite exhausting walk in the mounting heat, to find the venue which was on Royal Hospital Road. It was indeed, as forecast, a hot and sultry morning and by noon the temperature had climbed. But we managed the trek and arrived eventually, myself feeling a little bit worse for wear. I thought that from the outside it looked neat, and quite elegant in an understated way, but the place was not as big as I had imagined it would be. We arrived five minutes early to find the doors not yet open. They were unlocked dead on twelve and we were admitted but rather left to our own devices as the pre-lunch briefing for the staff on the day's menu was still happening. The waiters were all gathered in a corner of the restaurant receiving their instructions about the various specials of the day. I suppose that this was admirable for the knowledge they need, but we sat there like lemons for a full five minutes before someone tore himself away to speak to us. In my opinion that should have been over before they opened their doors. My first impression was of that briefing and the fact that for such a relatively small place (about thirty six covers) there were probably at least ten waiters and a maitre d', who was delivering the actual chat. This was an indication of the service level we were to expect.

To say we were a last minute booking, we were seated at a very pleasant table and not behind the kitchen door as might have happened in some restaurants. The restaurant gradually filled with eager diners, most very elegant and well heeled, but both Anna and I brush up well when we need to, so the company did not overawe us. The menus were presented, both the table d'hote and the a la carte menu, and the waiter told us what was specially recommended that day. For me, one of the most wonderful moments of any visit to a new restaurant is that moment when I cast my eye over the menu and learn what delights are in store. The description of each dish is as exciting, almost, as eating the food itself. Taking time over making that choice is for me, the equivalent to fashionistas trying on clothes in Harvey Nichols and trying to decide which designer outfit to buy this month. Anna and I perused both menus taking our time and sipping our pre-lunch Campari and sodas. We eventually both came to the same decision – we are only here once so let's go the whole hog, throw economic caution to the wind, and choose flamboyant, wildly expensive dishes from the a la carte menu, and ignore the good-value, but less exciting set menu. At this point the maitre d' arrived to take our order. He oozed charm and welcomed us to the restaurant and was personally very gratified that we had chosen to return. I did not correct him by telling him that this was our first visit, and put his words down to the somewhat obsequious style that he chose to use. We asked for more detail on some items then we spelled out our choices and sat back to await what we expected to be, perfection. There is something very elegant and grown up about sitting in a classy restaurant, anticipating the delights to come. For me there are very few things in life that I can get so worked up about – at least very few that I would mention in print.

A commis waiter glided to our table and set cutlery according to our order. One detail that always impresses me in good restaurants is that there is never the need to ask, "Who's having the fish, the lamb etc?" As the order is taken there is obviously some signal written down as to which diner has ordered what dish. I sometimes muse about what this sign must be. Is it something like "eld.W in r d" signifying "elderly woman in horrible red dress" or is it something as mundane as numbering the position of chairs at the table. Perhaps someone in the know will write and tell me. Whatever system they use at Gordon Ramsay, Chelsea, it works, and we were never once asked, "Who is having the …?".

Five years ago having a pre-starter was not the norm in local restaurants in the north, so the arrival of a small coffee cup of soup was interesting and unusual. The waiter told us it was vichyssoise with caviar, and we were instructed to enjoy. It was indeed delicious, creamy, full of flavour of the leek and potato ingredients, but most of all on a warm summer day, it is served cold and was wonderfully refreshing. It boded well for the rest of the meal. The show had started! The pre-starter had done what it was intended to do and had tantalised our taste buds into life ready for what was to follow. The next dish arrived, the real starters that we had selected. I had gone for Ramsay's signature dish – ravioli of lobster and langoustine served with a lemon and coriander sauce. Anna's choice was foie gras terrine, a delicious looking dish but somewhat against my own moral feelings towards the force-fed French geese. I am not a vegetarian in any way, but foie gras is one item that does not sit well with my conscience. However Anna was eating it, not me, so I concentrated on the sublime flavours of my own starter. We both agreed that each dish was well worth whatever it was priced at and sat back waiting for more.

The main courses listed on the menu had been many and various and as usual I had hovered between two or three before finally settling for the lamb dish. If in doubt about any menu, my final choice will always be lamb. In this instance I was to be served a combination dish of canon of lamb plus eight-hour, slow-cooked shoulder of lamb, which by all accounts would fall off the bone into its accompanying "puree of salsify, sweet caramelised shallots and spinach". No need to order additional side dishes then. Anna, ever the fish-lover, had selected roast monkfish and baby squid with asparagus and Savoy cabbage. By this time of course we were also well into our bottle of Californian red wine, neither of us being too worried by the "red for meat, white for fish" guidance. We drink what we know we like. As with most restaurants of this calibre, presentation is superb, and then next comes flavour and sheer appreciation of the love and work that has gone into each dish. Neither of these main courses disappointed in any way whatsoever, but our pleasure was slightly disturbed by the almost continuous attentions of the maitre d', who hovered too much in my opinion. By the end of our meal when he had interrupted our conversation at least four times to enquire whether everything was going well, I wanted to scream at him and tell him to leave us alone.

We had eaten slowly so as to appreciate the full effect of the food and the ambience, and now we were almost replete. But what is a superb lunch if not rounded off by a pudding? With only a small amount of room to spare we opted to share a *tarte tatin*. Then we had a lovely surprise. Pre-starters had been around for a little while but I believe this was the first time I had been served with a pre-sweet course, and it was such a sweet appealing item aimed at making the diners smile. We were served with a miniature cornet, filled with cinnamon and panna ice cream. It was only two mouthfuls but it was exquisite. Then our *tarte tatin* arrived looking exactly as this classic French pudding should look, with buttery-textured pastry and sweetly flavoured apples. Finally we drank small but double strength espresso coffees accompanied by handmade petit fours. I had to admit that the reputation that this restaurant has earned was well deserved.

The final action was of course to request our bill. We had enjoyed the food and wine now was the time to keep the relaxed expression going while looking at the itemised account and the mind-blowing total. £4 for a bottle of water struck me as too pricey, as did £5 each for coffee and chocolates, and the total of £186.70 was certainly at that point, the most I have ever paid for lunch for two. Was it worth it? On many levels, yes it was. We experienced a fantastic combination of seriously good cooking and sublime flavours and textures of food, but at the same time my conscience did prick a little at the amount that would have fed many families for a week.

17

Paradors, Pousadas, and Puglia

Pousada de São Brás de Alportel
São Brás

POUSADA DE S. BRÁS
2005
BUFFET DE S. BRÁS

Sábado – Jantar

Boas Vindas
Flute de Espumante com Sorbet de Tangerina

Couvert
Azeite Perfumado com Dentes de Alho e Flor de Sal, Azeitonas Temperadas com Alho, Orégãos e
Azeite
Oferta de Pão do Cesto

Buffet de Frios
Torresmos do Rissol
Peixinhos da Horta
Empadinhas de Galinha
Pastéis de Bacalhau
Rissóis de Amêijoas
Sonhos de Camarão
Estupeta de Atum
Salada de Polvo
Salada de Grão com Bacalhau
Salada de Tomate à Algarvia
Salada de Pimentos Assados
Assadura
Salada de Batata com Oregãos
Salada de Tomate com Queijo Fresco e Orégãos
Salada de Conserva de Cenoura
Salada de Alfaces
Sapateira Recheada
Carapaus Alimados
Presunto com Figos
Enchidos de Porco Fateados

Buffet de Petiscos
Favas à Algarvia
Berbigão com Alhos, Azeite e Coentros
Choco com Batata Doce e Ervilhas

Buffet de Quentes
Creme de Ervilhas com Hortelã, Figos Secos e Aroma de Presunto
Corvina de Caldeirada
Cabrito Assado com Batata Nova e Espinafres Salteados
Buffet de Sobremesas
Doçaria Regional
Queijos Regionais
Fruta

Café/Docinhos de Amêndoa

Preço/Pax: 22,50€
Iva 12% Incluído

Grupo Pestana Pousadas – Investimentos Turísticos, S.A.
Pousada de São Brás · Poço dos Ferreiros · 8150-054 São Brás de Alportel · PORTUGAL
Tel. (+351) 289 842 305/6 · Fax. (+351) 289 841 726 · recepcao.sbras@pousadas.pt · www.pousadas.pt

2004, and we had decided like thousands of other older British couples, to look for a house abroad where we could get away from the everyday rush of life here in England, and experience days of slower pace and the charm of a new environment. In England people talk about stress all the time so even if you seem relaxed you start to wonder whether you also might be stressed like everyone else. Admittedly the only deadlines we worked to were the catalogue printing and auction deadlines for John's business, but I hoped they could be relaxed a little. I had persuaded John about the benefits of having a house overseas and our ideal plan was to spend all the winter abroad but come back to our house in the UK for the summer — always supposing that we would have a summer in the UK. The spate of TV programmes was showing how to do it, or how not to do it in many cases. As John and I had both lived abroad for a limited time years previously, going overseas did not hold fears but we felt it did make us a little more realistic about how life could be.

For me the ideal was to find a small house in southern Europe, situated ideally in a small town or busy village. We needed to be in the midst of things and become part of local life, as well be able to keep in contact with everyone via email. John would continue to run his postal history auction business (dealing in old letters and postmarked envelopes) via the Internet, but on a slowed down scale, with perhaps two big auctions a year instead of the four or five that was normal. We had definitely decided that conurbations of houses where mainly ex-pats clustered together were not at all attractive to us. I still speak reasonably good Italian from my au pair days, plus school French and a bit of Spanish, and John speaks Spanish quite well from his days working as a courier and printing several books in Spain years before. He also has school French and German thrown in for good measure. We both love Greece, in particular the magical island of Crete, where we have spent many holidays, but as neither of us can say much more than "hello" and "thank you" in the Greek language, we opted not to look there. Speaking the language is in our view the top requirement after having enough money to buy a place, so we settled on the idea of looking in parts of Spain, Italy or even Portugal as our joint efforts in Portuguese had been OK, based on the grounding of similar Latin languages we both had.

This was not to be a "rush-job". Mistakes can be made that way. We decided that we would make those countries our destination for short holidays over the next couple of years and spend some time looking at houses and target areas while holidaying. The first trip we planned was to go to southern Spain and meanwhile I started looking at all the Internet sites to seek out estate agents who were dealing in sales of established village houses rather than new-build complexes aimed at the hoards of British and Northern Europeans making a mass exodus from their mother countries. I simply couldn't understand why anyone would want to live in a small enclave of mainly British couples who in general didn't mix with local people and who mainly had each other for company around a shared pool and perhaps at a local restaurant they adopted and took over. Why leave Britain for more of the same with only endless sun as the extra ingredient? But that's just my view and apparently there were lots of people who felt that was the ideal way to live. We just needed to know where they were so that we could avoid them!

We decided to base ourselves in an HPB apartment in the Costa del Sol, beyond Marbella, and hopefully a little more off the beaten track from the "all-day English breakfasts and egg and chips" hang-outs. We didn't do too well on that score, as this site turned out to be the first site HPB bought many years before and since that time the busy tourist strip of cafes and football TV bars had caught up with the place. Our apartment backed onto a bar that was noisy even in January, but as we were going to spend most of our days touring around it didn't matter too much. We were concentrating on looking around small inland towns such as Antiquera, and at villages within striking distance of the highway such as the road between the coast and Granada, so of course, as neither of us had been to Granada before, a visit to the famous Alhambra Palace was also on our must-do list for this holiday. As well as going to see the Alhambra we decided to combine it with another item on our travel wish-list – to stay in a Parador. These Paradors are luxury hotels converted from fortresses, palaces, convents and monasteries all over Spain. One of the most prestigious, where we were going to stay, is actually part of the Alhambra Palace, built in the fourteenth century as part of a mosque and later converted to a Franciscan monastery.

We decided that we would drive to Granada in the early morning visiting a few houses for sale on the way, then arrive at the Alhambra in the late afternoon and stroll in the famous gardens, saving the real tour of the palace for the next day. In late January there was little in bloom in the gardens but nevertheless they were still very charming, with elegant old trees and geometric hedges bordering sleeping flower-beds. Our room was furnished with heavy old carved furniture that looked as if it too had survived from centuries earlier, but it was exactly right to match the general décor and atmosphere. We went down for dinner looking forward to our meal as Paradors always reflect the best local food available in the region and with luck we would be able to sample the local specialities. This was indeed the case and we ate in the small but sumptuous dining room which had a magnificent coffered ceiling. The waitresses were in a uniform that was a version of local dress and looked smart but not too showy, and were a fountain of knowledge regarding the food on offer and its origins.

We started with *Gazpacho Andaluz*, a cold soup of that region, made from fresh tomatoes, cucumber, lots of garlic of course, and stale bread. It's one of John's favourites and it was good, although I have never really got the taste for eating cold soups, even on a warm evening. For the next course we ate *Pollo a la Alpujarrena*, a very garlicky chicken dish which comes from a very traditional almost primitive style of cooking based on local ingredients. This dish was accompanied by a mixed salad and beautifully cooked potatoes that were very yellow and melted in the mouth. Portions in that dining room were more than ample so we were quite full but I couldn't resist trying a local pudding. The one I chose was the quaintly named *Piononos of Santa Fe*, (apparently this was named after Pope Pio who was nicknamed Pio No No because he was so conservative). It was a custard-filled tart about two inches deep, with sugar on top that had been caramelised and was scrumptiously crunchy. Of course the local wine, a Tempranillo if I recall, was robust enough to stand up to the garlic we had eaten and therefore just right for this meal. We retired feeling completely satisfied and I then spent the next half hour before going to bed gazing out from our room window looking at the gardens in the moonlight and the lights of Granada, just down the hill. I didn't know the city well enough to pick out specific places but there were churches and tall buildings lit up and standing out from the rest of the town.

Our house search in that area led to nothing and in fact we had a narrow escape as we did find one house that we thought might have suited us if had we been prepared to do quite a bit of "making good". The house was unoccupied but still furnished when we looked round, and we learned that the young husband had been deserted by his wife and left with a very young child to look after. There was a tiny pair of white leather shoes on the floor in the front room that gave the place a very poignant feel. The young man had returned home to his parents instead of continuing in the house alone. A very sad story. However, luckily we decided to re-visit the place on our own as opposed to being accompanied by the house agent on our first visit. As we got near to the house we realised that there was a particularly awful smell coming from somewhere very near. We looked around behind the row of houses and discovered that there was a pig farm directly over the back of the property wall. We had not smelled it when we first visited and we even suspected that there had been an arrangement to move the pigs out of the way for the day so that we wouldn't know it existed. As this was January and the real heat had not yet arrived, one could only imagine what the smell would be like in mid-summer. Indeed it was a lucky escape.

We went on to look around the Algarve area of Portugal and although we did not find the ideal property there either, we did discover Pousadas, the Portuguese equivalent of Paradors, large hotels in beautiful buildings. The two we visited were very different. Sagres Pousada was a modern building stretched along the top of the cliffs with a view over the Atlantic, and in an area where, in its position at the western tip of the Algarve, it had been developed, by Henry the Navigator, as a seafaring training school. The other site was at Sao Bras, near Faro, and was a slightly smaller hotel built about thirty miles from the coast. At the Sao Bras Pousada we had a wonderful evening that we had noticed being advertised when we first stopped there for lunch. They were offering a full buffet menu featuring all the local dishes that were typical of the surrounding region, so of course we booked ourselves in for that gourmet experience.

I think we realised we were in for something special when we arrived and saw the huge buffet table in the dining room, lit by a fabulous chandelier above, and absolutely groaning with food. So many different cold dishes already were laid out and apparently more hot dishes were to follow. As usual we discovered that we were the only British guests, with local families and groups of friends making up the complement of diners. As we took our table we were served first with a tray of breads, about half a dozen different varieties, with little dishes of olive oil for dipping, green olives, and a tangy herb butter. I could have made a meal from these breads alone, but I tried to restrain myself and leave room for what was to follow. We then got up and went to the table and were shown that each area as we progressed around the table had a different type of starter. First the fish where there were plump sardines in oil, different types of fish roe, local salamis and chorizo, each dish bordered by flower-carved carrots in vinegar. Next came heftier starters such as chicken salad, very similar to our own coronation chicken, and featured rillettes of chicken with aubergine in a light curry sauce.

Then we moved to hot platters and first more fish – salmon fillet this time done as a sort of fish stew with broad beans and chorizo. My own favourite came next with pieces of succulent local lamb with a surprising accompaniment of sweet potato mash, and a side dish of a wonderful fresh mint jelly that was quite transparent. These savoury dishes, both starters and main courses, were accompanied by local Dao white and red wines from Casadio Santa.

We sampled almost every savoury dish before us, and then it was on to the amazing sweet buffet laid out on side tables. The southern Europeans tend to make sweets that are either cakes or flans, or fruit salads and ice creams, and this display was no exception. There was a Torta do Laranja (orange cake), Torta do Figo (fig flan), various fruit salads, fresh strawberries, and something that looked like eggs but was a type of sweet white pumpkin, although I didn't try that one. I suppose that from the start we adopted the policy of taking a small portion of as many dishes as we could, so that we could try all these local dishes, and by the end of the meal we were well and truly stuffed full. We sat at a table by the window, with a view overlooking the valley behind the hotel, and on that May evening there were dozens of swallows swooping and diving until dusk. It was idyllic. And if I remember correctly the whole menu cost us something like 28 euros- that was approximately £20 pounds at the time. What a bargain.

One of the traditional things we enjoyed in Portuguese restaurants was the little pot of home-made sardine paste that would always arrive accompanied by good bread to stave off the hunger pangs while you were waiting for the food to arrive. And in one local restaurant that we frequented we always arrived fairly early and were given this platter of bread and sardine paste, then it was a matter of waiting for the main dish to be ready, as most of the things on offer were cooked just outside the main restaurant doors in full view of the diners in a huge wood fired oven. This was the entertainment as well as the food. Our particular favourite was described on the menu as "kid in oven" which was not the disposal of some naughty child, but tender young goat kid that was absolutely scrumptious.

Our search for a house carried on through the next winter when we decided to take a short break in Puglia in southern Italy, an area that is largely undiscovered by tourists as yet. The area has some very unusual houses that look like traditional haystacks but made of stone, including the conical roofs, and painted white. They are called *trulli*, and there are lots around Alberobello (beautiful tree) town, a place that has been declared a World Heritage Site. We stayed at one of the converted old farmhouses in the area, a *masseria*, with foot thick walls that seemed to replicate a castle. The area is pretty basic in its amenities and we were sent off one day to look at the "amazing new shopping mall" that had been built about twenty miles away. When we eventually found it and went inside we found it compared more to what we know as a Cash & Carry, or Makro depot, but to the local people it was fantastic. With this type of experience in mind we decided that I would soon be very bored living there as all we ever saw women do was sweep the street outside their houses, or shop and cook. Certainly there was no social life for non-Italian women.

But we did discover another wonderful restaurant. We had to hunt for it and again it was in an unlikely place through the customary small business units of an industrial estate but then suddenly the road turned into a patch of countryside, and we knew immediately from the smart big Mercedes and Jaguar cars parked around that this was something good. It was called "The Fornello di Ricci". As we entered this family-run restaurant it seemed dark and foreboding, but after getting used to the level of light in the room we could see that it was rather like a hunting lodge with boars' heads hung around the walls, and old-fashioned wooden chandelier lighting. However the show of shining glassware on each table made up for the lack of light and we settled into our table for two, ready for the long haul. Looking at the menu the price seemed quite high for that area of Puglia where nothing ever costs very much, but by the end of our meal 50 euros each for the eight course tasting menu seemed remarkable for what we eaten.

We were first served with a glass of sparkling Spumante wine accompanied by tiny meatballs as an appetite primer – delicious. Then what seemed like a collection of starter courses arrived; there was a braised cabbage leaf stuffed and rolled, with a filling of cheese and rice mousseline, a very light and tasty dish; a small dish of lightly fried beetroot crisps; salt cod and aubergine balls which had been deep-fried; a marinated mixture of wild mushrooms and baby octopus; small slices of local salami, and at the end of this succession, a dish of greens cooked in stock and dredged with parmesan cheese. We worked our way through these appetising starter dishes, thinking that it was a meal in itself, and sat back in satisfaction. What would arrive next?

In Italy, particularly in the south, one or even two farinaceous dishes would now follow and that day it was gnocci (little potato dumplings) with ricotta filling and served with a pesto sauce. This sauce is made from basil leaves, ground pine nuts, and parmesan cheese and lots of good olive oil, and originally from northern Italy, near Genova, so I was surprised to find it here in Puglia. For some it may be an acquired taste but it is so fragrant and flavoursome. This dish was followed by a pasta dish of ravioli stuffed with fish and cooked in a fish stock with purple sprouting broccoli so it arrived at the table as ravioli in its own broth. Again it was such an unusual but wonderful combination.

By now we were thinking that surely we must be near the end of the meal, but no, we were served next with a pan-fried breaded veal chop in a fresh tomato sauce, veal being the most popular meat eaten in Italy. That really was the end of the main courses but still there was a cheese course with salted ricotta (this cheese can be eaten salted or sweetened), *scamorza*, which is a hardened version of the soft fresh mozzarella cheese, and the thinnest slices of Gran Padano which we know as parmesan cheese. Finally we were served a small plate of tiny sweet cakes not much more than a mouthful each, but everyone so delicious. Then as a *digestif* after such a huge meal, cup after cup of wonderful coffee. Throughout the meal our neighbours at the next table, a big crowd having a family celebration for their daughter's birthday, kept up a running commentary for us on the ingredients and the origins of every dish. They could not have been kinder. And I forgot to mention that good local red Pugliese wine was served throughout. I think that after that meal I didn't eat a food again for a couple of days as I was too full but it was one restaurant that I would love to go back to one day.

Our house hunting trips came to nothing as there were too many variables to take into consideration and when we found out John had cancer two years later I was very glad that we had not opted to live anywhere else other than at home. I still believe there is the best medical treatment in this country even if the NHS has a few hiccups. And I realise now that when you are faced with that diagnosis it means everything to have friends and family around you to lean on or to hold your hand from time to time. Living abroad we could not have had this support.

18

God's own County

Anthony's at Flannels

<u>Swine & wine</u>
Thursday 28th September

Pig's Head Terrine

Home Made Black Pudding
Salmon Cheeks, Pea Espuma

Pork Belly Cannelloni
Pickled Salad

Roast Cod
Ham Hock Ravioli's, Cider Apples

Butter Poached Pork Fillet
Maws and Lung

Golden Raisin Granola
Vanilla Ice Cream, Pedro Ximenez
Reduction

£60 Per Person,
Including four glasses of wine.

John and I have wandered around the UK and around the world experiencing some wonderful food but at the same time we were always fitting in little lunch or dinner trips to the tried and tested venues nearer to home. Over the past ten years or more the city of Leeds has been growing in stature mainly due to the ever-increasing activity in the finance sector. New skyscraper office blocks spring up where there were once down at heel parades of shops, and of course with the increased money in the city, has come an understandable demand for new restaurants. There is always a new kid on the block somewhere in Leeds. Sadly not all survive.

No 3 York Place is just such a restaurant and a haven that became a firm favourite with us both. Originally it was set up as Gueller's, run by a very talented chef who excelled in the kitchen but who in those days was not quite such an expert in running the business side of the operation. There were ups and downs and eventually Martel Smith, who we had already come across in his sumptuous but under-used restaurant at Gateforth Hall, took over the business with Dennis, his Belgian business partner, who ran front of house. We have had some wonderful meals there over the years including two Christmases when we have opted to dine there for our special Christmas Eve dinner. One of their specialities is a hot soufflé that varies seasonally in the flavour of sauce that is hidden deep in the centre. In summer it may be apricot or raspberry, in winter perhaps chocolate. Eating this pudding is a truly amazing experience as it manages to be feathery light in your mouth and yet eventually so filling that it's a struggle to finish. I do usually manage it though!

John and I gradually dropped into the habit of dining out somewhere in Yorkshire most Sundays, but we never solved the problematic ritual connected to it. It usually went like this; eat a light breakfast, read the Sunday papers, then one of us usually suggested that we could go out perhaps into the Yorkshire Dales and find a nice pub serving good food for lunch. The problem came in deciding where to go. We knew so many good pubs in all areas of Yorkshire, but when it came to choosing one we never were able to decide. We have always kept The Good Food Guide and The Good Pub Guide handy on the bookshelf, but we could never decide which one to go for.

There was a host of tried and tested places and I never understood why it was so hard to decide which place we made a beeline for each Sunday. Nevertheless if the suggestion had been made at eleven-thirty, mid-morning, it would always be nearer to one o'clock before we set off or if we managed to decide earlier, we would phone ahead to find that the restaurant was fully booked and so the discussion would start all over again. We loved the atmosphere and the food at The Crown, in Great Ouseburn, and they used to serve all day so that meant that if we couldn't decide in time to get to a pub before two o'clock cut off for food, we could always fall back on this place. They had a traditional menu with superb gammon and eggs served up on enormous plates. Then the management/ownership changed and although we continued to frequent the place and delighted in the new light and airy conservatory, it wasn't quite the same.

We have travelled far and wide for good food. One of the furthest for an evening meal is The Tontine, north up the A1 from Leeds, where they would be awarded my medal for the best mushroom risotto I have ever tasted. Another firm favourite for Sunday lunch, alongside Millbank near Rishworth and The Angel at Hetton, has been The Fleece at Addingham near Ilkley. This roadside pub is owned by Chris Monkman, who has been well known around the Ilkley restaurant scene for quite a while. When I was going through a rather unhappy period in the late eighties, I used to often escape after Opera Group rehearsal on Saturdays to his restaurant at the far end of the Ilkley high street, and sit there and read the papers, have a delicious light lunch perhaps of pasta or a salad, and gear myself up mentally for the week ahead. I'm not sure anyone knew of my bolt-hole but it meant a lot to me at the time. Chris Monkman then went on to own the Old Pool Court restaurant for a while until he then moved up to Addingham to this delightful pub with its stone flagged floors, mismatched chairs and tables, and its good honest approach to the menu. One of our favourites has been the whole roasted chicken, stuffed with lemon and garlic. It's a pleasure to watch the faces of nearby customers who have perhaps not seen the dish before and you can feel them thinking "Surely one person isn't going to eat all that?" Well there have been occasions when one person did eat it all, but the last time we ordered it, it was with the intention of sharing it with our grandchildren, Jasmine and Sadie, who are real fans of roast chicken. It's a good place to people-watch at The Fleece and a delight to watch the deliveries of plates of thick hand-cut brown bread served with soup, or the equally thick hand-cut roast beef wedged into doorstep sandwiches, piled high on a plate. Proof that it doesn't always have to be a gourmet feast to please.

This "surprise" routine that has developed around birthdays has sometimes given me a headache trying to find something different to do for John in September when his birthday comes around. One year I booked a short trip to Venice and my research on Google told me that on the very day of his celebration there was a "Festival of the Canals" with teams of costumed gondoliers racing each other, supported too by street gatherings where local folk cooked and brought out their offerings of home-made dishes. That sounded wonderful! We wandered up to a spot near the Rialto Bridge where some enterprising Venetian had roped off an area near his garage and brought out his dining chairs and was selling these prime viewing spots. As he wanted only a couple of pounds we decided to settle there to watch the races. Our local neighbours were so pleased to have strangers join them in their celebrations and explained everything that was happening to us in great detail. They also encouraged us to wander across the street to sample the local dishes and our absolute favourite was a dish of sardines in a sweet wine and onion marinade.

But I digress, as I wanted to tell you about one of the Yorkshire surprises that I decided upon. John likes to experiment with cooking, sometimes successfully, sometimes with rather odd pairings to my mind. So for one birthday I booked two places at the Cookery Masterclass at Hazlewood Castle, the imposing old place on the edge of the A1M and the York Road, near to Tadcaster. We had already dined there a couple of times and been quite well satisfied. The short programme began with the students (only half a dozen of us) meeting and chatting over a glass of champagne and a light lunch in the restaurant, before donning aprons and joining John Benson-Smith in his kitchen. By this time lunch service was over and the kitchen was a far less busy space, with cleaned-down, gleaming stainless steel worktops. We sat and watched every stage as he took us through a stunning dinner menu with one of us joining him in turn for a hands-on participation in the various steps involved.

We gradually learned the secret of producing a perfect *potato dauphinoise* to accompany the succulent pork belly braised in cider with red cabbage, then watched while we were shown how to sear plump scallops to perfection for the starter and to pare carrots and courgettes for its Asian style pickled garnish. But the *piece de resistance* was the perfect poached pear and chocolate sauce that ended the meal. After our cooking session the afternoon was rounded off with afternoon tea in the Pickled Pear café, a smaller basement off-shoot of the main restaurant. We had a wonderful time and I considered that was one of my most successful birthday present ideas. Later we reproduced the menu for all our friends as another fundraiser for our local hospice. I still think one of the best ways to raise money is to invite friends to share food and if the food is good enough they are always more than happy to part with cash. We hold a fund-raising Strawberry Tea every year and the word has now spread so much that we have trouble fitting in the fifty or so people who turn up into our small square patch of a garden, but it's always a great event.

In the last five years Leeds has seen the arrival of one of the rising stars of the restaurant world. In 2004 a new venue opened along Boar Lane, one of the main shopping streets. Anthony's seemed a modest affair from outside and when we ventured in to celebrate John's birthday in September we found a cool basement dining-room with minimalist décor and white linen dressed tables. The word around was that this young chef was something special and apparently had worked alongside the great chefs at El Bulli near Barcelona, the star in the European gastronomy scene. I hoped we were in for a treat and I was not disappointed. There was a standard lunch menu and a tasting menu, and as the latter looked really special and this was a special celebration, that was what we opted to try.

We were first offered a welcome cocktail of pineapple, fresh peas, blackberry and elderflower that was tongue-tingling and fresh with quick flashes of the different tastes zooming about in your mouth. Then followed a starter dish of what has become a signature dish for Anthony Flinn – white onion risotto with coffee espresso at the base and parmesan air on top. It's hard to explain what explosions of different tastes fight to have precedence in your mouth as you eat it, but I think that element was my favourite in the whole meal. The next course was poached quail with chickpeas, white beans and croissant veloute – in other words a small portion of soup, but again such a unique combination of wonderful flavours. A tiny portion of langoustine and pig's cheek garnished with almonds and apple slices next, followed by an equally beautifully cooked piece of monkfish in avocado cream with delicate beetroot ribbons. Each plate was a work of art as well as a triumph of flavours. The dish which could be regarded as the meat course arrived next, a delicately roasted squab (pigeon) with artichoke, green peas and peanuts. All of these combinations are so unusual but only this particular dish was one that didn't work for me and I found it a little cloying on my tongue, but well worth trying and tasting. Finally if the meal had thus far been unusual, the sweet course was very, very different. It was sweet cucumber ravioli – each fine sliver of refreshing cucumber rolled around a filling of sour cream ice cream and garnished with demerara jelly and sugar – stunning in it's refreshing mouth cleansing appeal. We then rounded off with lemon chiboust – a lemon barley ice cream with lemon sorbet. We were pleasantly full but not overloaded because all of these dishes were presented in small taster portions, but perhaps knocked out by the complexity of the meal. We were served coffee with petit fours and even these were superb – a chocolate with pumpkin oil, a real sugared jelly and a piece of tangerine chocolate ganache. That was certainly a birthday lunch to die for. We have often lunched since at Anthony's second restaurant above Flannels clothing store, again in Leeds, and have sampled the unusual dinner events such as a Cheese night, where every one of seven courses featured cheese in some way, and I can't help but admire the Flinn family, who are certainly developing a food empire to be proud of.

Another firm favourite that I have to mention is the Crab and Lobster near Asenby, a good half-hour drive from our home. I first went to this pub more than twenty years ago when it was owned by Jackie and Dave Barnard, a couple who had previously started a small restaurant in Boston Spa. Jackie had a real eye for creating an unusual atmosphere and entering this pub for the first time people would stand there, open-mouthed, taking in all the antique paraphernalia scattered across every shelf and surface and hanging from every point in the ceiling. Many places have emulated this style since then but she was the first to risk what we might call a "shabby-chic" look today. As the pub name hinted, they specialised in fish dishes and firm favourites were the pint of prawns – a traditional pint-glass tankard filled to the brim with succulent shell-on prawns and accompanied by wonderful home-made aioli, and their basket of just baked bread – and second favourite, the fish sandwich, triple layered with smoked salmon, poached salmon, cooked white fish, prawns and again home-baked brown bread holding (or almost holding) it all together. A crowd from Opera Group would usually meet to celebrate New Year's Day there, long before I met John, but we have still continued to frequent the place as a couple in the last few years. Unfortunately the original owners departed for Majorca, and since then it has changed somewhat but still is well thought of. In fact I have been there so many times over the years that I have joked that when I go (and I'm not intending departing this world just yet), I think my ashes should be discreetly scattered around their gardens.

19
Changes

Melanzane Parmigiana

(aubergine stack)

1 large or two small aubergines
2 buffalo mozzarella balls
120 ml olive oil.
2 oz parmesan to grate
400 gm tin chopped tomatoes
1 medium onion chopped roughly
2 garlic cloves chopped finely
basil leaves
half teaspoon dried oregano
salt and pepper

Slice the aubergine(s) into ½ inch thick pieces and fry in a pan in the olive oil. Turn regularly until brown on both sides and remove from the pan to cool (this will take 10–15 minutes). With residue of oil in the pan sweat the chopped onion and garlic slowly until transparent but not brown or charred. Add the chopped tinned tomatoes, salt and pepper to season, and the oregano. Let this cook slowly for about 15 minutes, topping up with a little water if the mixture seems to be too dry. Assemble the cooked aubergines and sliced mozzarella by alternating each one around an oven-proof casserole dish. Pour over the tomato sauce, then strew the top with a few basil leaves and cover the surface with a layer of grated parmesan cheese. Cook the dish in a medium oven until thoroughly hot. Serves 2–3.

Over the last two years life has radically changed and John and I can no longer be regarded as "the foodie couple". After John came out of hospital, with his surgery scars and radiotherapy burns needing to heal, for many months food took on a different format. For at least six months the main piece of equipment in use in the kitchen was the food blender. I strived to get as much taste as possible into blended versions of thick soups made with mushrooms or carrots and swede, or trying to produce ultra-smooth shepherds pie and liver and onions. Those months compared well with the years of child-rearing when culinary masterpieces were replaced by sausage and chips, boiled egg and soldiers, and the ever perplexing question of how to get vegetables into the diet. It's a period in your life when there doesn't seem to be any point in cooking complicated meals when there is nobody to share eating them.

I even sent a couple of recipes to the " Head and Neck News" a photocopied publication that the hospital sent every couple of months giving help and support to its patients. After surgery, the aims are always to keep the food intake constant and make sure that the calories mount up by adding cream and butter with no real regard for the former healthy eating rules. If you can only eat small portions of food three times a day then it has to be high calorie food or body weight starts to suffer. From the accounts that we read and the patients we still see at hospital clinics, John has fared better than most. His re-gained speech is regarded as exemplary, and our menu of meals has gradually extended to a small but reasonably interesting repertoire. Unfortunately for me that means eating a bit more fish than I am happy with, as fish is so much easier for John to eat than meat. In fact his meat-eating days are over. So we now have a few good recipes that we both enjoy, *melanzane parmigiana* (a tasty dish of aubergine slices, mozzarella cheese, and tomato sauce topped with parmesan cheese and baked in the oven), ratatouille made with red and orange peppers, onions and tomatoes and topped with an egg fried in olive oil, salmon fillets in all guises, and perhaps a surprising choice – duck legs in plum sauce. For the rest of the time I'm afraid we have to eat separate dishes as I can eat lots of salads and vegetables which John struggles with, so he falls back on prawns and avocados at least three or four times a week.

The biggest change has been the sweet course – puddings! Before the operation John never ate chocolate or cake or anything sweet at all. Now his sweet taste buds seem to have come to life and his favourite food is anything from the dessert section at the supermarket. Chocolate anything – cheesecakes, mousses, trifles, cakes with cream – all are more than welcome, while a dish of *tiramisu* will disappear in two minutes. It is strange how his previous taste preferences have disappeared or become non-viable and have been replaced by this urge for sweet things.

We do try to have a meal out from time to time but it only works if there are a few of us to cover the gaps in conversation. If we dine out together it tends to be a very silent meal (John is unable to eat and talk at the same time) and it takes a fair while to get through even two courses, by which time John's food is cold. So after some discussion between us we decided that I might carry on going out to restaurants but with a different set of people. I miss the whole experience of eating out at good food places too much to leave it behind forever so over the last year I've found a compromise.

Every month or so I meet with a group of ladies who have come together courtesy of Woman and Home magazine and their idea for supper clubs. These clubs run now all over the UK, and the rules, if there are any, are made by each particular gathering. Our group, now the White Rose Supper Club, chooses to meet in restaurants while some may meet in houses and take turns to cook. Whatever format they adopt, they are all, like our group, ladies who like to meet and eat. When I joined I found I was at least ten years older than the rest of our group but that has never been important and I now look forward to getting together with these new friends each month. And more recently a few female friends from our Opera Group set have started to eat out together too, so I now have a couple of dates a month which satisfies my foodie side.

Life has changed totally but the main thing is that we are both still here, both now reasonably healthy, and our family and friends are around us. Instead of following food pursuits, we concentrate on theatre-going, and Sundays are mainly dedicated to endless games of Scrabble! Life goes on.